M. Mosopala
12.07.07

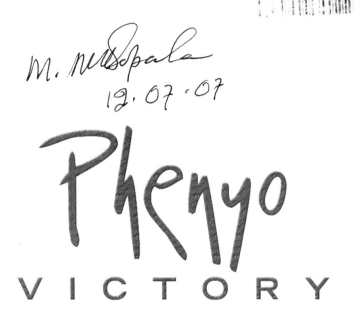

# Phenyo
# VICTORY

## MAGGIE BOPALAMO

# Reach Publishers

...inspire the world with words.

Self-publishers and Distributors of all books

ISBN 978 1920084 45 5

Published by Reach Publishers, P.O.Box 1384, Wandsbeck, South Africa, 3631

Website: **www.aimtoinspire.com**

E-mail: **reach@webstorm.co.za**

Printed and bound by Pinetown Printers, 16 Ivy Road, Pinetown, South Africa, 3610

Edited by Greg Dardagan for Reach Publishers

Cover designed by Gareth Lagesse for Reach Publishers

# Acknowledgement

◆

I am grateful to many people who encouraged and supported me in the writing of this book.

First of all, my grandchildren who asked so many questions and inspired me to put pen to paper. My family were very patient and supportive as I spent many hours that turned into weeks that turned into months writing. I particularly thank, Solomon, my husband, himself imprisoned for three years during the struggle, who filled in gaps and details in my story. My three children, Kennedy Molefi, Olivia Magae, and Harold Lebogang gave me wonderful advice and encouragement.

Headman Matholo Motsepe, of Moiletswane was most helpful in providing details about the farm.

My thanks goes to Bishop Kevin Dowling of the Roman Catholic Diocese of Rustenburg who has been a pillar of support for many years; not only for me, but for many involved in the struggle in the Bophuthatswana and elsewhere in South Africa. In the most difficult days, he was a voice of the voiceless. Bishop Dowling and the priests of St Joseph's Mission, Phokeng, selflessly opened the church doors offering asylum to those fleeing the Bophuthatswana Police. Times were difficult.

Many others were helpful and supportive, always there with advice, and practical assistance. I would like to thank the Tsholofelo Community for offering space to work in silence for which I am most grateful, particularly to Sr Georgina and Brother Joseph. My parish priest, Fr Anthony Padua, generously accommodated me in his tight schedule to render assistance when required. Br Finbarr Murphy, sometime of Phokeng and now of Nairobi generously gave up holidays to do the enormous initial editing. In addition, Fr Stephen Giles proofread, suggested amendments, and put final touches to the manuscript before it was sent to the publishers. To these, and many others unmentioned, heartfelt thanks.

# Foreword

$\blacklozenge$

Africa is rich in its people and its proverbs. A Kenyan proverb observes: "Proverbs are big messages in small words". The richness of our people and our proverbs is a never ending journey of discovery, a recognition that the wisdom of the people in its proverbs is a continuing lesson that will enrich us if we have eyes that see, ears that hear, and a heart that feels.

Our Setswana proverb: "Mmangwana o tshwara thipa kafa bogaleng" ("The mother of the child catches the knife by its sharpness") sums up for me so much of the life story of Maggie Bopalamo. Yes, a truly strong and courageous African woman, but whose strength can only be understood if you look long into her gentle eyes and see more, and if you listen to her words but listen more deeply than the words you hear. That is a mystery all the world needs to discover that peace and dignity cannot be found except through a courage that is lived in gentleness, integrity, and "being" fully a person in relationship with one's sisters and brothers, a relationship that continues even past death with one's ancestors.

Maggie came into my life in January 1991 when I began my ministry as a bishop in Phokeng, near Rustenburg, serving a wide area right to the Botswana border. I had been to this area many times before that but I had never lived there. Now in 1991 I was to discover the inner strength that has empowered Maggie's whole life as an "African woman" in the full sense and mystery and beauty of that term.

These years marked a critical period in the struggle for liberation and human rights in the "homeland" of Bophuthatswana. I sometimes feel, since the crucial first democratic elections in 1994, that not enough has been written or reflected upon in terms of the history of the struggle in the "homelands" as distinct from "South Africa". A unique story waits to be told about the wonderful human beings who responded to the challenge in the socio-political context of the "homelands", which in the case of Bophuthatswana after the attempted coup in 1988 was a context of oppression and gross human rights violations.

Her story in this book will trace her own very personal sufferings at the hands of the Bophuthatswana regime and its security forces. Maggie was one of many other unknown and forgotten women and men who were part of the "struggle" in Bophuthatswana, and who not only survived but became people with something special to give. I remember so clearly how deeply I was touched by these "little ones" when I gave my own testimony to the Truth and Reconciliation Commission hearings in Rustenburg. Some women told their story of being raped and physically abused by security forces in police cells in Bophuthatswana (Bop). Even though several years had passed the pain of re-telling those stories saw these courageous women breaking down and sobbing  but the pain did not and could not break them as women. The Burundian proverb puts it well: "The truth passes through fire and does not burn".

The story of Maggie's personal journey at that painful time will no doubt grip you as you read these pages. I will never forget the anger and disgust I felt one Friday morning when I heard how the Bop security police had picked her up at 5 a.m. at her home and she had simply disappeared. They had taken her away in her nightdress. I spent the morning going round various police stations until, acting on a hunch, I went to the Governor's offices in Phokeng, and in a building behind his offices I met one of the security police. I demanded to know if they were holding Maggie, and he admitted they were. I spoke in icy terms to him and made it clear that action would follow if they did not release her. After all, I said, she was a sick woman struggling with cancer. I went to her home to inform her family, and brought back her clothes and food the family prepared. The police refused to give her the food but they took her clothes. Next day she was released, but the exhaustion and strain on her face spoke of the toll this event, among many others, had taken on her. But such violations of her dignity never broke her. "When there is no enemy within, the enemies outside cannot hurt you"  an African proverb. Maggie was and is one of those "valiant women" we read of in the Bible.

And it is her personal faith which will also be revealed in the lines of this book. Her childhood remembrances, the influence of her family, the culture of her people, her involvement in her own faith community, her socio-political vision  these were some of the factors which played such an important part in the mystery of who she is, and why her life unfolded as it did. One can learn so much about one's own life and development as a person through the story of people like Maggie.

While she was deeply involved in the struggle for human rights and justice in Bophuthatswana, she was also part of the "struggles" of her own people. The story of the people of Phokeng will also, I hope, be told in some way at a future time. Maggie is one who could contribute so much to that story as well.

I hope that through reading this book you will in some way "encounter" this very special person, Maggie Bopalamo. The quiet inner strength, the radiant smile, the carefully chosen words, the ability to feel deeply for other people, the recognition that here I am in the presence of a wise woman, a true "elder" of the people these are some of the impressions I always have when I meet Maggie. "Truth should be in love and love in truth" Tanzanian proverb.

Our new nation is blessed to have people like Maggie who can guide us with the wisdom gained from a life in which there was much pain, but a life which was always rich because of personal faith and courage, and deep integrity. I trust that you will also be touched within your spirit by this eminently readable story of a life well lived.

Bishop Kevin Dowling
St. Joseph's Mission,
Phokeng

# About the Author

♦

Eighteen years ago, in June 1988, Maggie was still a lecturer at the Tlhabane College of Education. She enjoyed her work as Head of Department of African Studies and was passionate about her job and totally loyal to her calling of teaching. Little did she realise that what she valued so much i.e. education and teaching would be cut short prematurely. She could never have anticipated being in a prison for ten months.

A staunch and active member of the St. Joseph's Catholic Church in Phokeng, she was also affiliated to the African National Congress and was closely involved with matters of her community in Phokeng. However, she always felt a certain amount of freedom in the knowledge that she was doing nothing wrong. Regardless, her movements were followed very closely by members of the Bophuthatswana homeland Special Branch which ultimately resulted in her incarceration.

It's now many years after this ordeal and Maggie is enjoying her retirement from her job as District Manager of Rustenburg Schools and from Politics in the North West Province in South Africa. Phenyo Victory is the story of her struggle to serve as a reminder of the past. *"We should not forget for if we do, history has a tendency of repeating itself."* Maggie Bopalamo

# Contents

The OLD SOUTH AFRICA divided among four provinces.

The NEW SOUTH AFRICA divided among nine provinces.

# Part One

# **Childhood**

# Polonia, Oh Polonia!

◆

I am an African.

I am a woman of Africa, born into a Christian home where the traditional practices of my people were banned as pagan.

Polonia is in rural South Africa. I remember it as a hot, dry village of red dust which clogged the nostrils in the heat of summer. Polonia is found in the old Transvaal in South Africa. It was a place of sanctuary for many of the tribal people who wanted relief from strict laws, forced upon the people by the king and family members who followed cultural practices.

Polonia village was founded by the German Lutheran missionaries. These missionaries were ministers who, with their families, loved the people they came to serve in Africa. These men not only brought the Gospel of salvation of Jesus Christ, but also new hope in a troubled land.

Polonia is the place of my birth. I was born in the early hours of the morning, my mother writhing in pain in her bed. The room was full of old women who sweated profusely, adding to the natural heat of summer. The rains had last fallen four weeks previously, and the earth was scorched.

It was the 24th January ,1939.

According to the custom of my people, I received a name immediately: Mampee. This name does not reflect my real character. The translation of Mampee is: "One-who-continually-cries". But I have come to accept that I am a strong woman. I do not cry easily. I have been through many hardships and this has only strengthened me as a woman of the African soil.

Names are important for Africans. They reflect our roots and culture. The name that stuck by me is one I like Machinto. It has no meaning but it is the one my elder sister used as she was unable to pronounce another name given to me Ma-Gideon  Mother of Gideon.

It was only later in life that I became aware of the split life we Africans were forced into by the oppressive regime. This dual life was strongly reinforced by the missionaries who had little appreciation of the beauty of our natural African religion. When I was registered, I was given only "Christian names". These were names government officials could spell and names that indicated my place in the Christian community. Officially I am Magdalene Mirriam Bopalamo, but in reality I am Machinto Maggie Bopalamo.

Later in life, many people would joke with me about my year of birth. It was the beginning of World War 2, when Germany invaded Poland and the allied nations were all drawn into the war.

South Africans, black and white, went to the "Great War" as our old people called it. While Europe suffered under the evils of Hitler, South Africa suffered under the evils of Apartheid. World War 2 came to an end in 1945, the year of my brother Abram's birth.

Apartheid would be terminated only 49 years later, after a protracted struggle. I never dreamt of the pain I would go through to help bring liberation to my people and my beloved Africa.

I was born into a family of six siblings. Our eldest sister, Suzan, was born in 1929. Next was a son, Behrens, born in 1933. The third child was my sister Midah, born in 1936. I was the fourth of the family and the youngest daughter. One of my younger brothers, Lazarus, was born in 1943. Abram, the youngest, was born in 1945.

Later we discovered my mother had given birth to another child. Ironically, this painful information was revealed at my mother's funeral, when one of my uncles told the mourners there were actually seven children in our family and not six as we had assumed all our lives. There had been a boy who was born just before Behrens. His name was Matime. He had died as a baby.

I grew up in Polonia. Being poor, we were taught from an early age to be productive in the community. But the same as any family, we siblings had our own fights especially with the one who was born just before or after. With us girls it was always the question of whose turn it was to wash the dishes, or to cook. Fetching water was more exciting. You would meet friends at the mission pump. We queued, and as we waited for our chance to pump the water into buckets, we played around. As we carried the water on our heads like graceful dancers, we planned to meet again for more games. For us this was much more exciting than washing dishes.

Fetching wood was a bit risky because we encroached onto the farms of the Afrikaners around us. Sometimes they would chase us. During such days we went home without wood. But things could get even worse. One day, together with two friends, Meisie and Mamputu, I decided to fetch firewood from one of these farms. That day, we made one mistake: we invited an older woman to join us. We had frequented this area on several previous occasions and had escaped with wood. On this particular day when the owner of the farm came upon us, we ran for dear life leaving the older woman behind. She could not run as fast as we could. She was caught and arrested.

At school the following day we were busy in class when the police arrived. The principal led them straight to our room. We were summoned to the police station and asked to bring our parents along. Our class teacher Mr. Mahuma was very angry with the police. But there was very little he could do.

At the police station, every parent was given a stick to give her daughter three lashes on the buttocks. My father gave me three very mild strokes. The mothers of my friends were shaking with fear since they were unable to cane their children. They feared that the Afrikaner would punish the girls! They requested my father to administer the strokes, and he obliged. Then the policeman made us promise repeatedly that we would never again trespass on that farm for firewood.

The older woman was fined £5, about R60 today, but in reality the fine amounted to several months' wages.

My father was very strong. We never went out to get wood after our ordeal with the farmers. He did that for us. He carried big logs whenever he came back from the farms, where he was employed. He would cut these into manageable pieces for us. He was always the first person in our house to wake up. He made the fire and put water on and only woke us up when it boiled, so that we could make tea.

My father did not depend on public transport when making journeys to family and friends. He walked and he was a fast walker. If he asked you to accompany him, you'd be running all the way or you'd be left behind.

I remember when my younger brother, Lazarus, lay in a hospital in Pretoria after breaking a leg while lifting a water tank. The tank had fallen on to him, fracturing his leg in several places. The hospital managed to mend the leg. I was to accompany my father to the hospital to visit him. He could easily have taken a train up to Pretoria station and got transport from there to the hospital. But my father had his own ideas. We alighted instead at Hercules, which my father referred to as the "cement station", and walked all the way to the hospital!

I persevered because of my anxiety to see my younger brother. I was so afraid that my brother was going to die because of the manner in which the accident was explained. He was not staying with us when the accident happened. He was living with my maternal grandparents, herding the cattle and goats. He and another cousin had gone to fetch water in large iron tanks, using a small cart drawn by two oxen. Lazarus had been instructed by our cousin to sit at the back of the cart and hold the tanks (full of water) in position so that they would not slide and fall. However, the tanks were too heavy for him. When one of them had started to slide, he could not stop it. In his attempt to hold it, he had gone down with it. Once on the ground, the tank had landed on one of his legs breaking it in several places.

As black children, we had no such facilities as sports grounds, swimming pools or tennis courts. We had to create our own games and fun. Among the games we played with our peers was diketo. This was a simple juggling game played with small stones. We would scrape a little hole in the ground. Sitting around, a player would throw a stone in the air. Before it landed, the same player, using the same hand, had to grab a stone from the hole. If you missed it would be someone else's turn.

Another type of diketo used several shallow hollows dug in the ground. The game was similar to chess.

We also played kgati. Two girls would hold a rope and one or more of us would skip on either side of the rope, taking care not to touch it. African-Americans now play it with two ropes at once and call it "double-dutchie".

There was also a game, which was similar to hockey except that we used crooked sticks and an empty tin! One day during a match a player released the stick by mistake. It landed on my leg with terrible force. I fainted and woke up at home. The girls had carried me there.

We played basketball at school, different from the popular American version. We enjoyed it so much that even outside school hours we would go to the grounds to play. Basketball was not as modest as netball. You could jump freely and if you wanted to play it rough, you could kick your opponent at the same time as you jumped to field the ball.

Games were fun, but religion was taken very seriously. Our parents were true believers who hung on every word of the German missionaries. Polonia was a German Lutheran missionary settlement situated near the headquarters of the Bakgatla Ba-Mmakau tribe, between Brits and Pretoria.

The residents of Polonia were originally members of the Bakgatla Tribe who left their ancestral homes because of pressure by parents who forced their daughters to marry men they did not love. The Lutheran missionaries would then receive such people who had fled to Polonia for protection. They would take them through Christian rituals before converting them to Christianity in the Lutheran tradition. Polonia thus became a kind of religious asylum.

The name Polonia puzzled me. It was not African as far as I could figure out. It was only later in life when I had the pleasure of visiting the former communist countries of Eastern Europe, through the good offices of the South African Council of Churches, that I learned something about this strange name. In Poland we visited the house bearing the name Polonia - the Lutheran missionaries had studied there before embarking for South Africa.

There were very few households in Polonia. In actual fact there were 58 families and all were staunch Lutherans. The church building was a white structure conspicuous by its size and beauty among the simple thatch-roofed houses with their mud walls.

Our houses were surrounded by a high outside wall which formed an enclosure, totally hiding the house and giving privacy to the family. This enclosure was the lapa; this is where guests were received; family meetings took place here and sometimes even the preparation for supper. This was the pattern in all households, an obvious influence of the German missionaries who inculcated in the residents that they should not be seen from outside as they went about their household chores. It was all about privacy.

Sunday church attendance was not an option. It was central to the value system and no-one chose to depart from that rule. There were two services every Sunday. Morning service ran from 10am to noon. After this service we were free to go home for lunch and to visit our friends. We children used this opportunity for playing.

The second service would start at 3pm during which time all people would abandon whatever they were doing. When this bell rang which was audible at a distance, no-one would dare stay away. This service would last till 5pm.

At the age 15, we started Confirmation classes. Instruction took two years. We were confirmed when we were 16. It was taboo to miss a Confirmation class or any of the church services. During the first year, classes took place on a Monday; we referred to it as Mandaga. Throughout the last year classes took place four times weekly, Tuesday to Friday.

Besides learning the catechism "off by heart" we performed regular chores at the missionary's house which included cleaning, drawing water, fetching wood, working in the kitchen, doing the family's washing, and working in the fields where we weeded and gathered the ripe vegetables and fruit. These we brought to the house, prepared them for sale, or bottled them. Such tasks were not an option for us, but a must; they were accepted as part of our preparation for Confirmation.

Manual work at the school was always done on Fridays. We went to draw water from the river, which we used to scrub the floors and clean the windows. We also attended to the teachers' houses. But the water always beckoned us. Instead of taking buckets of water back to school, we would sneak into the river for a swim, hoping not to be discovered. Returning from the river we would be made to line up. The culprits were easily detected by their pale, ashen faces. They were assigned to a classroom where they were sjamboked.

The same thing happened on Sundays between the first service and the second. We would rush to the river immediately after lunch, to swim. The lure of forbidden fruit would be so overwhelming that we altogether forgot our responsibility and thus missed the second service

Monday morning at school was 'interrogation' time. Who had missed church yesterday? Who bunked the second service? The first one identified was enough. Polonia was a closely-knit community. Each one knew everyone else, their standards at school, their homes, their siblings, their ages. The first culprit would sell out on the rest of us. Then the whipping would start, administered by the principal with the assistance of one or two teachers. You had to be ill to miss a church service.

It was only after my marriage that I began to lose interest in the Church, but I soon came to my senses. My husband was not strict about church services; I soon realised that I had to take the lead. Church attendance had become part of me; it was my Polonia upbringing, no doubt.

Revisiting these events, I smile to myself. These were good, innocent days of hard work, strict parents, of a clearly defined religion, of friends who stood together and supported each other.

But when I allowed my feelings to surface, I was left with many unanswered questions: Why do we blacks have so little, and the white farmers and the missionaries have such smart things? They have running water in their homes, electricity, carpets on the floor, an electric stove, a car. These thoughts and feelings of puzzlement could not be readily expressed in those days in the presence of an elder or a white. It was perhaps my dawning of critical consciousness. Later on, I know that as these thoughts broadened into more adult questions I was able to vocalize them and take a stand.

Growing up in Polonia, I now realise what a loving family I had. Certainly we were poor; but we had each other. My father was a quiet man, who loved to smoke his pipe. Christened Daniel, he preferred his Tswana name, Ramphephethu. He worked on various farms as a labourer. He was of medium build, but because of his manual work, he had become very muscular! It was his duty to ring the Church bell for the various services during the week. This was a job reserved for strong men!

My mother was a loving woman of faith. She was called Maadimo a name 'Something-borrowed-must-be-returned'. She too was quiet but with iron in her resolve which was fuelled by her faith. Her constant refrain in times of trouble was Modimo o teng. O tlaa re thusa. 'God is here. He will help us.'

Mother worked as a domestic in Johannesburg. This meant that she had to spend most of her days at the home of her employers. We her family only saw her once a month! But our mother made sure that our education was taken care of.

I remember when times were really tough and we could not pay our school fees, mother would hatch a plan with her employers that if they paid the fees, she would work for months without any pay. This they agreed to. So for many months she did not have a penny in her pocket, and could not send money to us back home.

My eldest sister, Suzan, was ten years my senior. She was unfortunate to be in school at the time when mother was sickly. Because of her illness, mother was forced to spend a lot of time in hospital. Suzan, being the eldest, could therefore only study up to Standard Five as she soon took the role of Mmarona (our mother), in the house.

She became an expert dressmaker. Sewing and knitting were a sideline business while her main work was that of a domestic servant in Johannesburg. She could do many beautiful things with her hands. She would go into town and meet someone wearing a beautiful dress. She would then buy the cloth and reproduce the pattern from memory. Suzan was blessed with two kids - a daughter Debora, and a son, Julius.

Suzan died in 1981. She suffered from flu but postponed a visit to her doctor, thinking the illness would pass. Without concern for her own welfare, she continued working.

One afternoon, on her day off known as "Sheila's Day", she visited my aunt at her place of work. "Sheila's Day" was Thursday which was free for domestics; they could attend Church or visit each other. The white employers had agreed to this, so that their domestics could serve them on a Sunday. When Suzan came to my aunt Fini's place of work, she even discussed her flu. She told my aunt that she had had the flu for some time but that day she intended consulting a doctor. My aunt left her resting in the room, and rushed to the kitchen to prepare a quick meal for them both. She was gone for less than an hour. When she returned, Suzan appeared to have fallen asleep. Fini spoke to her, but Suzan did not respond. She shook her, but there was no life. Auntie could not believe what instinct was telling her. She called her boss. A doctor was summoned but Suzan had gone to her reward.

Suzan had one surviving child, Deborah. Today Deborah is employed at a school where my sister Midah had previously taught before retiring.

My elder sister, Midah, attended a Catholic boarding school, Notre Dame Secondary, near Roodepoort. She passed her Junior Certificate and later did the Higher Primary Teachers' Course. She was a teacher until she retired in 2001.

Midah was blessed with two daughters, Maureen and Yvonne. Maureen is a teacher; Yvonne is a fashion designer and lives in Mozambique with her Canadian husband.

Behrens, our eldest brother went to boarding school at Bethel Training

College in 1950. In 1952, his last year at the college, a student riot erupted and the school was burnt to ashes. Dissatisfaction with food had sparked the riot.

The boarders said they had been served samp contaminated by worms and claimed they had found snake tails in the beans. Behrens was named as one of the ringleaders and he and other students had to serve six months' hard labour at Leeuwkop Prison. Their sentence took effect in mid-winter, and years later they would recall having to fill wagons with broken stones before dragging the load unaided. They were barefoot and the sores on their feet needed hospital treatment.

Coming out of prison, Behrens found a job in Johannesburg. But his health was affected and he was never strong and robust like his father. At the time of his death in 1990, he was employed at Rosslyn Industries. He was survived by his wife Regina, two sons and a daughter.

All his friends, many of whom had not gone as far as secondary school, loved Behrens, calling him "doctor" mainly because he was always up to date with current news. He loved using big English words when he talked - terms such as cantankerous, stupendous, marvellous, came easily to him. We ordinary folk would describe a window as a hole in the wall to allow in some light. But this would not satisfy Behrens. To Behrens a window was an orifice in an edifice for the admission of luminary particles! He had a bombastic style of humour; but the intention was to entertain rather than to show off.

When you related a story to him, he would listen attentively and ponder gravely. His response could be very philosophical. He would posture: "Let's suppose you lie", or, "It doesn't make sense to me".

Behrens was always proud of me and boasted to his friends about my academic achievements. I respected him greatly. I wished so much that he could have made it academically. He did not intentionally mess up his life. He took his studies seriously. But circumstances at his school made it all difficult for him and others. The judge's ruling at the arson case was also unfair. Some of his accomplices were released and readmitted to the same school. Others were released because they were under age, while some, presumed to be ringleaders, were refused re-entry.

My younger brother, Lazarus, is a teacher and a very good singer. He was blessed with three children sons, David, a mechanical engineer, and Tshepang an officer in the navy; and a daughter, Tumisang, who is still at school.

Our youngest brother, Abram, is a Lutheran minister. After some years as a pastor, he and others broke away from the mother church. They established the Reformed Lutheran Church. He is presently the bishop, but works only over weekends. During week days he is employed at Home Affairs in Mabopane, and in Brits. He is blessed with three daughters, Boitshoko, employed by a travel agency in Pretoria; Tshegofalang, a computer engineer specialising in networking and computer technology; and Kgotsofalang, who is still at school.

Back in the 1950s, my father, being of the old school of thought, was not in favour of allowing girls to be educated. He believed they should marry and be housewives; or at best, work as domestics! My mother was a woman of vision. She believed in the equality of women, and encouraged all her daughters to get an education.

*Maggie while at Ndebele College Of Education.*

# Cattle And Other Memories

◆

My paternal grandfather bought a farm where he spent the greater part of his life. He seldom stayed at Polonia for any length of time, preferring Rankotea as the farm was called. The Afrikaners called it Krokodilkraal. There was a hut there where he stayed. Sometimes grandma would join him for short periods when there were major tasks to be performed.

Grandpa kept cattle, and he also produced good crops of mmopo, maize. When the crop was harvested and the grain separated, he put it into bags and brought it to Polonia for us. We always exchanged mmopo for maize meal at the mill at De Wildt. Sometimes a whole bag of grain was taken there to be ground for us.

Mmopo played several roles in our domestic economy. We could sell a bag for money and use the money to buy other necessities. We would have these bags stored and used in this way until the next harvest. At times grandpa would send us madila, a kind of sour milk, which we ate with pap. Delicious!

Some days when schools were closed we visited Krokodilkraal and stayed in the hut with our grandparents. There was a lot of milk to drink. There were some Afrikaner farms next to grandpa's. They needed our fresh milk while we wanted their coffee, tea, sugar and bread. So we would barter our buckets of fresh milk in exchange for these groceries. The old boere bread cut in with large slices as a favourite. Sometimes they even provided jam with it.

With such an abundance of milk, we did not have to depend on diluted coffee. We boiled the milk and coffee together. It was not uncommon for the sugar to get finished before the other items. Grandma called coffee without sugar bitter-kofie.

Milk was also a source of cash at the farm. It was sold as curd at times from which grandma made butter. Bread was available only on days when there was milk to exchange at the Afrikaner farms; or if someone went to Brits to buy flour. The butter was also used as a form of body lotion or cream.

With the flour, grandma made fat-cakes, bread, dumplings and diphaphatha. This latter kind of bread was cut into small portions and baked on a wire grid that was supported by a three-legged stand called a drie voet. The fire was kept low and the thin chunks of dough were turned over to cook well. This bread was very tasty. The flour had to ferment before any of these could be baked.

There were always two types of dumplings. One was made with flour only while for the other, flour and maize meal were mixed and fermented. The dough was put in a dish or in small brown paper bags, which were so common in that pre-plastic era. It was left to steam in a pot of boiling water but care was taken that it did not touch the water before being fully cooked. This kind of dumpling was known as mantebelekwane.

Today most of our traditional foods are sold in restaurants in towns where black people buy them already cooked. You have to wonder what has become of us! First we renounce our traditional way of life and copy other people's traditions, then we buy from them the very food items we ourselves should be producing!

Beans also featured on our menu in the form of soup to which we sometimes added grandma's homemade butter and ate it with pap

There was also a lot of chicken. Boys and girls never ate eggs because it was taboo for children to do so. Since the adults never explained why eggs were denied us children, we had to make our own assumptions. We girls believed that adults did not want us to be prematurely fertile! We started to menstruate at 15 years of age.

When a chicken was slaughtered, we cooked the intestines in empty tins on the fire. The other parts of the chicken we ate were the feet, head and neck. When adults dined on meat, we kids would be satisfied with milk.

Going to grandpa's farm was a form of outing for us. It broke the monotony of life at Polonia. Next to where grandpa kept his livestock was a new village where people had just started to settle. Here there was a small primary school, which went as far as Standard Five. Successful pupils journeyed on foot daily to Polonia to complete Standard Six. It was quite a distance but people did a lot of walking those days. There was no public transport.

Uncle Philemon, my father's younger brother, and his family lived at this village. Philemon was the twin brother of Aunt Maria. He was interested in caring for grandpa's livestock and in crop farming. My uncle did not believe in educating his children. His admiration for grandpa's wealth of livestock approached adoration - another case of golden calves!

He wanted all my brothers to go herding livestock, but my mother intervened decisively. She wanted her boys to be educated. When grandpa became too frail for farm work my uncle preferred to nurse him at his own house instead of allowing him to return to Polonia to his own home. Grandpa thus died at the farm and was buried there. No-one but uncle knows what ultimately happened to the livestock. I am not sure what my father's other siblings thought about this, but in my family there were hardly any ill feelings. We still respected our uncle and visited him. In fact, the question of cattle never arose in our conversation. My brothers had other interests.

We were, however, taken by surprise some years later after my father had already passed away. All my grandpa's family members were called together and told that platinum had been discovered on the farm and beneficiaries would receive annual royalties.

My grandpa had six children and thus six households had to share the little given to them.

I'm told my father's uncle was also one of the buyers of the farm but because he did not have a family, he was reluctant to pay for it. Grandpa took over paying for it and finishing payment on his behalf. The result was that my father's family got two shares. Recently they made arrangements for three families to be grandpa's beneficiaries, and the other three to be their uncle's beneficiaries. In our family we have decided to save this money. We use it only on whole family occasions, such as funerals and tombstones. The last tombstone was that of my mother, which was unveiled in December 2004. We still have Susan's and Behren's tombstones to unveil.

Uncle Philemon died in a mysterious manner. He went missing while looking for cattle. The whole village including schoolchildren were sent out to search for him. After a week he was found "drowned" in the canal that runs from Hartbeespoort Dam, through Moiletswane and Brits, to Krokodilkraal. A post-mortem examination revealed that drowning was not the cause of his death. He was murdered before the body was thrown into the canal. To this day the mystery of his death has gone unsolved.

Ntate-mogolo Abbiot and his family departed this world in rapid succession. First, the second son died in a car accident leaving behind his wife and two very young sons. Next to die was mme-mogolo, their mother. She collapsed one day while weeding the garden. Then the last-born who left a family of three girls, was next to die. Then it was ntate-mogolo's own turn. That death left only the first-born who had raised his family at Rankotea, grandpa's farm. He was the last of that family to die.

None of my father's own siblings are alive today, but a large brood of children, grandchildren and great-grandchildren survive him.

On the other hand my Uncle David survives my mother's family. He is suffering from chronic arthritis. He's now aged 80. Both he and his wife Lydia are ex-teachers. They have managed successfully to educate their children. The first-born, Tsholofelo, a daughter, is a social worker with a Master's Degree. She is employed in a prison at Brits. The second-born, Thabo, a son, is an electronics engineer. The third-born, Shele, is also an electrical engineer. The fourth is a magistrate in Rustenburg. The fifth is daughter Mammy, a medical doctor specialising in anaesthetics. The sixth, Dineo, also a daughter, is a medical doctor at Klerksdorp Hospital. The seventh, a son, Itumeleng, is a librarian at Medunsa.

Presently Uncle David is father to our ever-expanding extended family. As family elder he listens to all our tales, whether of woe or of happiness. It is such a pleasure to have him still alive and making his wisdom available to us. He is now a priest in the African Episcopal Church. He and his wife are very actively involved in church matters.

An enigmatic personality, he succeeded in maintaining an apolitical stance throughout the struggle years. Yet he visited me regularly at Rooigrond Prison where I was detained. He still phones me daily to find out how I am keeping. He does the same with all his other nieces and nephews. Whatever happens to any of us in our large family circle, he will report by phone to the rest of us. We are not the only ones who enjoy the love of this couple; they reach out much wider. They are like social workers.

My mother had six siblings. Aunt Ephenia, the second-born and came just after my mother. The third-born, Uncle Robinson, left behind a family. The fourth, Uncle Behrens also died leaving behind three sons and two daughters. Uncle David, the only one surviving is the fifth. My aunt, the last-born, died early in life leaving behind four sons, Jeffrey, Lazarus, Kopi and Molefe, who now have their own families. They were cared for and educated by my eldest aunt before her death. They also have an only sister, the last-born, Sara, whose mother died when she was only three months old. She is presently a social worker in Rustenburg. At the unveiling of her mother's tombstone she was overcome with grief. Not having known her mother, she cried bitterly at the graveside.

As a social worker Sara hears cases where a person says: "I am an orphan and I have a problem." I was in their office one day when a social worker asked the complainant how old she was, and when she lost her parents? She was eighteen. They pointed out Sara as a real orphan, one who had never known her mother.

An interesting thing about both my parents' homes is the farm that both their parents bought separately. As fate would have it, the farm Moiletswane bought by my maternal grandfathers, has just been discovered to stretch as far as Rankotea (Krokodikraal), the farm bought by my paternal grandfather. It includes Elendsrus, the new suburb of Brits, and covers the Industrial Area including the abattoir. Furthermore, it extends to Mothutlung and Damonsville. I am told it also cuts through a great part of Mmakau. It is the farm which is about to be returned to us and other beneficiaries whose grandparents were also buyers. It is interesting to discover how little we paid for the farm in those days and how much is being claimed back now. There are also prospects of platinum being present there.

The final stage will be when Land Affairs officials arrive at the place where the community has been resettled to officially hand them a title deed. This community was not originally Bakgatla-Ba-Makau, when they bought the land. They came from different places. My grandfather and the majority of the people there, who are all related, came from a place called 'Monyamane' which is not far from Pretoria.

During those years people who owned land were forced to be under the authority of a chief. Thus the community was forced to be part of Bakgatla-Ba-Mmakau. With the present developments they have officially excused themselves from the authority of the Bakgatla-Ba-Mmakau Tribe. They call themselves Bakgatla-Ba-Moiletswane. They have even sent a strong warning that their affairs should no longer be discussed at that level.

Two council elections will be held shortly. One council will take control of the rural area and the other council will take charge of the suburbs. The elections will not take the form of a poll as is usually conducted in South Africa. Every family will send a delegate who has the competence to serve in the council. One would imagine that the council will be unwieldy, but that will not be the case. Taking into consideration the number of real buyers, there are not that many and each one of us falls under the name of one buyer. Under my grandfather, it is my mother, her children and grandchildren. The same with all my mother's siblings. All of us falling under the name Lazarus Motiang have to delegate one person. All delegates from all families will then be divided into Urban and Rural Councils. We have a leader assisted by an interim committee, not a chief.

My family has to see to it that one of us is present at all regular meetings, to safeguard our interests and to give the rest of us feedback.

The other families are my mother's maternal and paternal uncles. They also came from Monyamane to buy the farm. Others are my paternal aunt's families. All these people have their own beneficiaries. There are still other families. The majority of this community are in some way related and inter-married. For example, some of my cousins are beneficiaries twice, through both mother and father.

My childhood spent among this community was a very pleasant one. I found the people were close-knit, very happy and supportive. What a change from Polonia which by comparison suddenly appeared to me as artificial, dull and boring!

So when I left Polonia I was highly motivated to go to high school. I thirsted for knowledge. I felt this urge to really move forward with my education. I knew that I was changing, growing, and becoming a person who was moving beyond the restrictions of my roots and culture.

But at the same time romance was making itself felt!

For many years I had been aware of a young man who was interested in me. At first, when I met him, he was just Behrens's friend. Behrens seemed to have boasted to his friends about the achievements of his little sister. On this particular day I was taking grapes to sell in Brits. Polonia was rich in different fruits, and to earn some pocket money, we would collect as much as we could, and travel to Brits to sell it. Well, that day my friends and I boarded a train for Brits at De Wildt station. Here we met this young man who was interested in us.

Solomon, we discovered had been at the same school as Behrens and took a real interest in me! In my mental diary, this became 'my day of grapes,' the day I first met the man I was to marry.

We were to meet again in Mamelodi where my school had gone for a sports competition and debate. Solomon's college had been asked to act as adjudicators and he seemed to be interested in me. But my cousin Kgogo Motiang, who was also studying in Mamelodi, was very protective of me. He refused to let Solomon get even close to me. So we parted not even speaking to each other.

Our next contact was through the post. I had gone to my mother's place of work in Johannesburg and found a letter for me from Solomon. It had been written a while back and recalled the times we met in the train and at Mamelodi. I got the impression that a little frustration was brewing, and wondered at it. Solomon also updated me about his completed educational courses, and the fact that he was to begin teaching at Hebron.

I replied to his letter. Almost immediately he came to visit the family. But when he arrived at Polonia, I was not there. My father sent my younger brother Lazarus to accompany him to my maternal grandmother's. I had been staying there since it was still holiday time. So we finally met!

Because of the long distance, we could not meet very often, but Solomon was very persistent in his courtship. In 1957 while I was still busy with my education, our families met and discussed the possibility of marriage. Such consultation belongs to an ancient custom of my people; it underlines the fact that it is not just two people who marry, but two families who are going to be bound together in the marriage. Our uncles and aunts met to discuss lobola.

Lobola is the "bride price" or dowry which is paid to the bride's family. Many Westerners think that the man "buys" the girl who then becomes his possession. But it is not so. Lobola has different layers of meaning. In the first place it is a sign that the man is capable of supporting not only his wife, but also the extended family. Thus gifts are given to the in-laws and the aunts and uncles.

Lobola is a sign of honour bestowed on the bride. It reveals the value that is placed on her, not as a commodity but as the future mother of future members of the tribe. Again, lobola is a token of thanks offered by the groom's party to the bride's parents for raising a woman capable of living in his family and contributing to it.

Solomon's family offered £80 as lobola. Today the amount would run into tens of thousands of rand. When lobola is paid to the family, everyone celebrates because in reality this is the wedding day. Later, another ceremony takes place in the church for the blessing given by the minister.

*Award Ceremony Maggie, Dr Molapo and Mr Ntshabele.*

*Grandpa and grandmother, Amos and Maria Chengwe with one of their grand children.*

# Cooking

◆

Recently, my sister, Midah, and our cousin, Martha Maadimo, named after my mom, re-visited the way we were brought up. The discussion was really humorous when we recalled instances of our childhood at home.

During those days, we had to cook when school was out. Cooking then was different from what we find today. Food usually took a longer time to cook then than now. Pap and spinach, morogo, did not take too long. But if it happened to be meat that had to be cooked, you had to have the pots boiling earlier than usual.

Sometimes at Moiletswane potatoes were peeled and added to the meat. But we had to make sure that a lot of water was added for gravy. We were given small pieces of meat and a lot of pap and gravy. When the food was ready, I would dish out the porridge for everybody. An older person had to be called to dish out the meat. This was not the case with morogo.

Meat was always prepared in a smaller pot than the one for porridge. If there was some left over, the pot was hung up on the rafters. It would be served for the next meal. On days when we kids found ourselves alone at home we could do silly things. We would climb a chair, get the pot down, and cut a little portion from each piece of meat. We were clever enough not to take whole pieces as they were usually counted. The reality was that meat for kids was a favour and a luxury. Our diet was usually pap and fresh or sour milk.

Tradition demanded that adults be served first, starting with grandpa. Children were served last. Only after serving everybody could I sit down to eat. But then one of the children would already be asking for more gravy. The chorus would then start for more gravy, gravy. Ultimately I would sit down to eat my cold meal. Cold or warm, it was the same. It was all food. At one time, I happened to be the only girl among all the boys in the family at Moiletswane.

On days when we were going to have chicken for supper, we started by chasing the one that was identified. Then the boys would cut its throat before they put it in a big dish of boiling water to remove the feathers. When it was clean, it was cut open to remove the innards. A paper was lit and the whole skin was singed to remove the remaining fluffy hairs. Then the meat was cut into pieces, washed and put into the same pot to cook. We had to clean the intestines, for that would be the only portion left for us kids.

We cooked this besides the fire in tins. If we were lucky enough we also got the claws, the head and the neck. Adults had the whole chicken to themselves with different parts allotted to each in accordance with age. The remainder of the chicken was hung up again at the same place. When adults were gone, we would lower the pot and carefully remove what we could without causing suspicion. Should you be caught red-handed doing this, you'd wish that you were never born.

Not that there was any scarcity of food. It's just that forbidden fruit is always that bit more tempting!

Apart from the fresh milk, which was used in the tea, there was sometimes condensed milk. The tin was opened a little bit on either side. You had to measure it with a teaspoon to add to the tea. Because I was always the one sent to make tea, I had to fetch the tea leaves, the sugar and condensed milk from the main house. Before coming out of the main house I would suck a little bit from the condensed milk container. For us kids, condensed milk was a delicacy, compared to fresh milk. This is perhaps the reason why most of us who grew up those days, don't want anything more to do with the condensed product. We prefer the real thing.

Sharing in those days was the norm. A person arriving at mealtime was always offered a plate. If it was a child he or she ate with other children from the same plate. There was always enough food.

During wedding feasts, a large dish was prepared for children. We ate together from this dish. We knew after this we would be sent away to play or join those who were watching, or dancing with the bride and groom.

Grandma always brought a lot of delicacies from weddings.

Food prepared for weddings was the same as that prepared for Christmas. Later when we grew up this food was served even on Sundays. Today in most black households such food is enjoyed daily. How times have changed!

We played adult roles outside with other boys and girls. We would make a fire and cook improvising our own utensils. Those whose mothers worked in Johannesburg had play materials like dolls and plastic cups, saucers, kettles, spoons and dinner plates. grandma was always ready to offer a little bit of what was available to go and play outside. We would make a feast for ourselves and dish out the food like our parents did, serving the boys first, and calling them fathers.

We were conscious, however, of the right time to go back to our different homes to do the household chores and be available for errands. But when the boys and girls formed groups of singers and dancers, which went around the village, I did not join these groups. Nor did grandma encourage me. Yet when they were around I always watched them with admiration. If there was one good thing with youngsters at Moiletswane it was singing in their different groups wearing colourful Scottish skirts. This was youthful recreation at its best. There was no liquor served. Singers were offered home-baked cakes and cool drinks. They just enjoyed entertaining the community.

Apart from wedding feasts, there were also stokvels, almost every Sunday. Here you also had food as on Christmas days. But you had to pay for it. The aim of a stokvel was to make money. We went there with plates to buy the food. If the vegetables included beetroot, the dish was regarded as special.

Baptism and confirmations were occasions that were celebrated with special menus. These were rare. That is why at Christmas we children suffered occasional tummy upsets and milk was the usual remedy. The stomach ailments happened because of the unusual food we had in abundance on those rare occasions.

Added to the Christmas meal were jelly and custard, cakes and cool drinks. Children also had sweets to top it all.

As youngsters we excelled at household chores. We were taught responsibility and this prepared us for adult life. We also played a lot outside. Thus we were given time to exercise and socialise with other kids. We did not discriminate among our play mates. Sharing was a major part of our upbringing. We shared food in our homes with other children. Grandpa was like a headman sitting outside under a mimosa tree engaging the neighbours in discussions about land, or life in general. It was our duty to see that these adults had tea and when it was mealtime that they were also served.

People never made appointments. They came in as they pleased. If grandma or grandpa or both, were absent, they would repeat their visit. We just knew that our grandparents were away. They did not tell us. When they arrived, bringing green mielies or "morogo", we would then know that they had been to the fields. Sometimes friends and relatives came at night to sit there and talk, until we kids went to sleep. They called this practice go itisa, meaning spending time together after the day's work.

Those old people seldom got tired. They were not easily taken ill. I do not remember any instance where either grandma or grandpa went to consult a medical doctor. They also knew what to do when their cattle or goats were sick. I do not ever remember an instance when a vet was called to treat their animals.

Our grandparents had a natural wisdom and insight into many things. And they were equally focused. They knew exactly how to plan for the future. They had time enough to sit together as men in a kgotla to organize their lives and their community, to use their God-given talents to collectively sort out any problem.

Everybody had a role to play. In the evenings as adults got together for discussions. Young men, my brother Behrens's age would be outside singing beautifully. Their voices were so beautiful that even now as I write, I yearn for those tunes that they sang in the twilight. The music filled the whole community as darkness fell, and as we sat around fires we would listen with appreciation.

It was like harvest time when we teenagers of the time went to remove the chaff from the cobs of mielies. This we did in the evenings. As we worked, throwing the dry chaff on fire, which burst into big flames, we also sang our teenage lyrics. Besides singing, we posed riddles to each other. During such times the owner of the house would make us tea with sweet potatoes or fat cakes.

Behrens loved riddles, which would sound funny even today.

Can a doctor doctor another doctor who is doctoring other doctoring doctors?

We could not solve it and so he delivered the verdict, "Yes!"

Another riddle they loved: Cape Town is near the sea. If you remove the 'c' what remains?

We thought of the sea at Cape Town, and thus missed the pun. But the answer was Ape Town.

Then there was another one: The two-legged, go and get out a two-leg-legged from the three-legged so we can eat.

This meant, child get us a chicken from the three legged pot and give it to the people to eat.

Even at school as teenagers we enjoyed these riddles and tongue-twisters. It was an interesting kind of entertainment.

But I wouldn't say that parents and teachers of those days mistreated us. I know the youth today will condemn the previous generation for abuse. They will charge that it was a violation of rights especially those of the girl-child. But when I observe the problems modern parents have with kids, I appreciate what our grandparents did. Some of the youngsters today cannot even make their own beds, let alone wash dishes or cook. Some of them will admit that they don't know how to cook pap.

And what is happening to the young men who used to sing so beautifully in the evenings? Today you'll find them in taverns! That's their first port of call before going home from work. What about the boys and girls who spent time entertaining the community with their singing and dancing? Today they are parents before they know it! And what of those who acted out motherhood roles cooking with tins, playing with dolls? Today we have drug addicts. Others are being molested inside and outside their own homes. Yet others are kidnapped and used as sex slaves.

Thus, the safe society of yesteryear has turned dangerous, unable to protect its own children. Children are no longer seen as children and society has turned its back on them. No wonder they have lost respect. Traditional courts have long since ceased to function because communities have no trust in them.

Where do we go from here? I suggest we must plan our second liberation. But let's not complain too loudly - it's so early in summer!

# To Climb A Tree, Start From The Ground

◆

Next to the Lutheran church was another building, equally important to the villagers; this was the school. Officially called Polonia Mission School, it enrolled pupils from Grade One, formerly known as Sub A, through to Standard Six.

The church and the school were almost one in purpose and in administration. They were mutually supportive and interdependent. The missionary was the superintendent of the school and from time to time he would make his visits to assess the quality of teaching and learning. All teachers were expected to play prominent roles in the church.

The Sub A teacher, Mr. Dedrick Montoedi, an old man who had taught most of the parents of the pupils, was also a member of the church council. Both young and old feared him. When you met him in the street you wished you could escape, or maybe disappear. He was generally known as titchere yo mogolo, the old teacher. You would think he was the principal of the school!

Whenever the Sub A teacher corrected our slates, his son-in-law, the principal, Mr. Modiga, would be standing next to him. The old man's remarks compared parents and offspring: "This one is a block-head like the father," or "This girl is even more brilliant than her mother".

Once I talked to my Grandmother about this old teacher when I got home, and my Grandmother made it clear to me that we were not respecting an elderly gentleman who was even older than herself. To her, age was honourable, unquestionably honourable.

The principal taught Standard One and Standard Two. Another teacher, Mr.

Phillip Mahuma, fresh from college, taught Standard Three and Standard Four. He acted as choirmaster at school during assembly and also at church. The Grade Two teacher was usually a woman.

Shortly after I started Grade II, we received a new woman teacher whose name I cannot remember. The new teacher was very different to the former one in many respects. She made our lives unbearable.

The teacher would sit on a chair holding a long whip. You would be asked to stand next to her and she whipped your feet. In fact she always kept this long and sharp whip with her wherever she went, and used it to punish us, even for minor offences.

One day after prayers, this teacher summoned me to the classroom. This time she not only whipped my feet, but the whole body. The reason for my punishment, alleged the teacher, was that I did not close my eyes during prayers. I might well have done that, but I could not remember.

That day I cried forever. During break I did not play. And at the end of school I went home still crying. At the tender age of nine, I felt the injustice perpetrated against me. I asked myself how this teacher could possibly have noticed my open eyes when everybody was supposed to have closed eyes.

Arriving home, I thought, today I have a case for my mum to tackle, and threw myself on the bed and cried hysterically. Well, all mothers would want to know what was wrong with their dear child. I related my tale of misery and did not forget to include the logic about the fact that the teacher could not have seen my open eyes while all were at prayer. Does this mean that she does not close her eyes when praying? This must be so, or how did she see me.

My mum kept on exclaiming and sympathising but never said a word to indicate the teacher was wrong. I was never as disappointed as I was that day.

This unhappy incident taught me the lesson that such men and women could never be wrong. They were so high above the law that parents would only see the fault as that of their children and never with the teachers.

Young teachers from college were usually responsible for the morning parade when we marched to assembly. There, uniforms and general cleanliness were checked.

When I was in junior classes, there were two rows, one for the boys and the other for girls. A tall boy and a tall girl took the lead as we marched. Our teacher loved to conduct the morning parade in Setswana chanting La'nja la molema, meaning left, right, and left, right.

Before getting to the assembly hall, we had to pass through a narrow entrance towards the courtyard. One row had to go first. This meant the boys first, so that they would occupy the back rows at assembly. The leader of the boys was Biesie; and Martha Bulonga led the girls. So the teacher continued with his "la'nja la molema, la'nja la molema!" and would command, "Biesie tsena, Martha Bulonga, change your step".

As we played at home, we liked to mimic this teacher conducting the morning parade. One of us would play teacher while two others would play Biesie and Martha. We would burst into laughter when she issued the command, "Martha Bulonga change your step, Biesie tsena!"

Another teacher, a son of the soil, Fred Sefolo, taught Standard Five and Standard Six. He assisted at church on Sunday by leading the hymns.

Besides the children of Polonia, there were pupils from other villages who attended this school. They attended because of their affiliation to the church and they joined the confirmation classes. They also attended church on Sunday. A third group came from neighbouring farms.

These were times when we younger ones looked up to the older pupils in Standard Six with envy, especially when they wrote final examinations. On such occasions you would see a number of school inspectors, as well as the missionary himself, roaming the school grounds, all appearing very busy and dignified.

Indeed the missionary was an important figure, both in the village and school. He hired and fired teachers. The teachers employed at the school had to belong to the Hermansburg Lutheran Church and they had to be or appear to be - of good conduct.

We looked up to our teachers with the greatest respect. When they visited pupils' homes they were offered the best food which was served from the best utensils. Families went the extra mile to show honour and gratitude to these "learned" men and women. Every home looked forward to receiving a teacher in their house. The cynics advise that a man with one eye is king among the blind!

During the late 1940s and early 1950s when I was at Polonia School, there was a feeding scheme for pupils. Sometimes we were fed with soup and bread. We had to bring mugs and spoons from home. On certain occasions the menu was tea, and bread with either jam or peanut butter.

Women from the village alternated in preparing the soup and tea. Older boys had to collect bone marrows from the butchery at De Wildt in the afternoons. When the soup had been served to all scholars, the bones and remaining soup were given to the boys who had previously fetched the ingredients from the local butchery. Behrens was one of these boys at one stage. We always looked forward to days when he would return home loaded with a vessel of thick soup and bones which still had meat on them.

Our Standard Five teacher's favourite subject was arithmetic. In the morning, we started with "mental arithmetic" and those who did well would be shifted to the back seats. Those who fared badly, apart from being beaten with a very sharp stick, were moved to front seats.

I happened to be very good in mental arithmetic and a very fast thinker. You had to think very fast only ten minutes for ten problems. This made me a back seater most of the time.

Bright pupils who worked fastest and had all their sums right were selected to cut the bread that we ate at break. I had the honour of cutting bread and winning extra slices as a reward. When bread was left over, the principal asked questions and anyone who got an answer right, was awarded an extra piece. As I was one of the fastest learners, I was a frequent winner.

Our Standard Six scholars went to boarding schools when they passed. The majority of them went to the Bethel Training College, as it was a Lutheran institution. Others went to Kilnerton in Pretoria, Wilberforce, Botshabelo in Middleburg, St. Thomas in Johannesburg, or elsewhere.

The whole village always looked forward to the departure and arrival of students. They were the pride of the village. On their departure, most of the villagers accompanied them to De Wildt station. The same custom welcomed the new arrivals. They looked beautiful in their smart dresses and their plaited hair. They could speak good English and they helped us in school choirs when they were on holidays. Most of them were also good singers. We naturally looked forward to being students ourselves one day. They really paved the way for us.

My father, Daniel, was born and bred in Polonia. He went to the same primary school I attended, and was taught by the same old man who was my teacher in Sub A. My mother, Martha, however was born and bred in a village called Moiletswane, not far from Brits. She attended the local primary school.

My mother was born in the African Episcopal Church and after marriage she had to undergo confirmation classes to be accepted into the Lutheran Church. She became so captivated by the new denomination that when we grew up, we could never detect any traces of her religious origins. She was thoroughly converted.

My early days were spent between Moiletswane with my maternal grandparents, and Polonia with my paternal grandparents. Moiletswane was a very different place to Polonia.

The Moiletswane community was happier, freer and more flexible. Children there went to school in the morning, but those who herded the goats would not return to school after short break. It was a given rule. Those who cared for siblings when parents went to work in Brits had the liberty to bring them along to school. When I was in Standard Two, I went to school with my cousin Machekela, who was then nine or ten months old. When he cried, or was hungry, or the nappy had to be changed, I would go out to help him.

Because a number of us girls had to perform such duties, we would leave the toddlers playing under a huge tree in the schoolyard, checking them at intervals. The community of Moiletswane loved their school and teachers, and supported them. My grandfather's cattle kraal was attached to the school fence near the residence of the teachers. In the morning when the boys went to milk the cows, the teachers brought their containers to receive their share of milk, on a daily basis. When teachers departed for a weekend, we looked after their residence.

The most common religious denomination in Moiletswane was the African Episcopal Church. My maternal grandparents and all their family members attended this church. They probably brought it with them when they relocated from Monyamane, their previous residence. There were several priests at this church. During the service, they all took front seats. The singing was impressive. This congregation had been part of the Anglican Church before it was Africanised. They use the same hymn books as Anglicans. Each one of the pastors in front had a role to play. While one started hymns, another would read from the Bible. There were several readings and chanted prayers like The Lord's Prayer and Psalm 23. Then preaching would start.

A humorous incident happened one day as we listened to the sermon.

Pastor Rapula asked: "Tell me and don't be afraid to answer - can a corpse eat?"

Being just a kid I didn't know what led him to this question. I was not attentive like most children in church. But like most children I understood that this question was not really meant to be answered. There was silence for some time.

Then Pastor Modise unexpectedly answered; "Yes, you fed…while he was dead".

Pastor Rapula turned to Pastor Modise and asked "Modise, are you mad?"

"Are you also mad?" replied Pastor Modise.

Calling him by name, Pastor Rapula retorted: "Can you say I'm mad in church?"

"But you also said I was mad in church. Why?"

The argument was escalating and the sermon deteriorated into an argument in front of the congregation. It was amusing to see two men of the cloth in a heated dialogue and there was general laughter in the congregation until finally one elderly woman intervened with a hymn to stop the undignified episode from descending into a scuffle.

I never forgot this story. I related it to my mother many times. She loved the story and would laugh her heart out. She would remark: "Maybe they had taken a drop too much before coming to church."

At that early age of my life, I sensed that there was something unpleasant afoot regarding land. Land was being taken away from people although they had bought it and were the lawful owners. During those days blacks were denied the right to own land. Land was placed in trust of the nearest chief. He then agreed with the government to have the black community removed from the land and re-settled. The land they were forced to abandon was fertile while the new land was arid, and far from any town. Some opted to seek jobs in Brits and were prepared to walk to work, while others cycled.

Everyday we kids listened to grandpa and other elders of the community discussing their land, which was to be taken from them. They employed the services of a lawyer in Brits called Mareé. We picked up the name as "Maria". I always wondered who this Maria was, who had become the talk of the community!

My mother's maternal uncle was the cleverest of all the elders. In a way he had attained a level of education higher than all of them. As community spokesman, it was his task to consult Mareé. He could walk incredible distances and return home with a newspaper protruding from his back pocket! He kept the community updated on current affairs.

Later in life when I was a secondary school student, I read his defiant statement in the newspaper, "If the community of Moiletswane is to be removed, it will be over my dead body."

Sadly, die he did. However, then and only then, was our Moiletswane community forcefully removed to a very dry area called Dipompong.

All my siblings had stayed at Moiletswane with our maternal grandparents at one time or another, assisting with herding cattle and goats. We girls helped grandma with household chores. Grandpa and grandma had very busy schedules. There was never any time they idled. Midah herded the goats for some time while at primary school. She would leave school at playtime like the other boys and girls who had the same farm duties.

Milking was usually done early in the morning. The cattle kraal was opened just after milking time and grandpa would lead the cows and goats to the veld. Later in the day the boys would relieve him. Although I did not herd the goats, I was taught by Midah and my cousin, Kgogo, how to milk them. You kneel down on your left knee, and put the goat's right hind leg under your right foot. The goats had to be milked before their kids were released to suck. Calves and kids were kept separate from their mothers until milking time was over.

One day after Midah had locked up the goat kraal, she rushed in looking very distressed and shocked. Her clothes were in tatters. She had wounds all over her legs and hands. She had been savaged by dogs while trying to scare the goats out of someone's property. Grandma was very angry. She viewed it as a deliberate act by the owner who always released his dogs just when children were driving their animals out of his property. She was not going to tolerate such violence, and that farmer had to pay for letting the dogs loose on children.

Grandpa was a real farmer. On the fields near home, he alternated crops. As a result of such crop rotation, his yields at harvest time were impressive. He alternated maize, sorghum, vegetables, sweet potatoes and beans. There were times when manure was dug from kraals at home and carted to the fields to fertilize the soil. He had another field a distance away near the canal that got its water from Hartbeespoort Dam. In this field, besides maize, he also planted fruit trees.

The soil of both these fields was a black turf. There was a vegetable that grew among maize crops on turf soil. It grew on its own and we called it phare. It looks and tastes like cucumber, although it is softer, when young. We liked it and ate it raw, adding a pinch of salt. The leaves of this vegetable were cooked. Some liked it best when served with milk. Another vegetable looked like a green pumpkin and we called it leraka which when cooked on its own and taken with milk was very tasty.

On Saturdays, I would ask grandma to allow me to pluck phare from the field near the canal. We filled it in baskets and walked to Brits to sell it to the Indians. They loved it. It was used to make their archar. If you were lucky, they would buy the whole basket for half-a-crown. Sometimes they would bargain and start off by offering just a shilling, or a shilling and sixpence. Of course we too learned to negotiate.

By the time your bundle of phare was purchased, you would be really tired and hungry; the only thing you thought of was food. There was a café near the railway, owned by an Indian. They served fish and chips. All we could afford to buy was half a loaf of bread, and crumbs that remained when fish was fried. Opposite this café was a general store also owned by Indians. It had a very large stoep. This stoep was a popular meeting spot. People sat there to rest and to eat. We would sit in the stoep with other children on a similar mission, and enjoy our half loaves and crumbs. If funds allowed, we managed even a bottle of cool drink. Then, off we trekked back home with empty baskets and full tummies!

On reaching home, we would surrender the remaining change to grandma. She was very strict with her mielies. If for some reason you cheated by also plucking and selling maize cobs she would know. She would know exactly how many cobs you had grabbed. Now that I can analyse them with the benefit of hindsight, I realise my grandparents were very intelligent! When corn cobs were missing they knew when it was a thief from outside, or when it was one of us. In my own case, grandma would not even investigate; she would reveal to me exactly what I had done. Her orders were simple: "Stop that!" Thereafter, I was wary every time I visited the fields of encroaching on forbidden fruit.

The last-born of our family, Abram, did not stay at Moiletswane. The only time he stayed there for any extensive period was as an infant. My mother had fallen seriously ill and was taken to hospital in Pretoria. The hospital was then known as Pretoria General Hospital. Abram was still breast-fed. On the day mom was taken by ambulance to hospital, Behrens and I were instructed by grandma to take the child to Moiletswane where he would be fed with milk. Behrens and I set out on the journey; he carried the baby on his back. He was also pushing a little wire cart, which boys made those days. On this cart he had our belongings and also a little maize, which he was going to sell at the mill in order to buy us bread. Abram slept all the way. Polonia was three hours' walking distance from Moiletswane.

As we approached Stefans Station, dark clouds were looming and it was obvious a storm was on its way. There was a shop along the road which people called Ben's Shop. The shop owner, a Jewish man called "Mr Ben", and his employees must have seen us passing by with a baby on my brother's back, and me, a little girl of six, walking beside him.

With storm clouds threatening, they sent someone to call us back. We were taken to the back of the shop where Ben's wife started to ask questions about where we had come from, where we were going, and where the baby's mother was. She held the baby and I sensed her anxiety. The sympathy she displayed scared me and I wondered whether it meant my little brother was dying. She warmed some milk and tried to feed him. He took the milk with difficulty. We were also offered something to eat.

Outside it was raining very hard and was now dark. We still had a distance to walk from there to Moiletswane. They allowed us to start on our way when the rain subsided, because they were afraid that it was becoming too dark. Between Stefans Station and Moiletswane is black, sticky turf, very difficult to walk on when wet. We trudged along, however, and by the time we reached our grandparents it was not only dark and raining; it was very late - they were preparing for bed. The baby was now a shocking sight.

The following day I heard grandma telling relatives who were at the house: "I hardly slept the whole night. I kept wondering whether the child was still alive. I had to put on the light and touch and turn him, to make sure he was alive."

News of our late arrival, the difficulties on the way, and having to be offered shelter made verbal headlines in the area.

Behrens had to return to Polonia for school. I stayed on to help grandma with the baby who soon started to regain his health and to eat well. There was plenty of cow's and goat's milk. In no time, I was carrying him on my back to play with other toddlers outside.

We stayed at Moiletswane for the rest of the time that ma was in hospital. I even attended the Sub A class although I was not of age. By the time I started school in Polonia, they would not allow me to do Sub B because of the age factor. I was made to repeat Sub A. I soon realised I had got a head start.

The question of my brother Abram's health because of mom's hospitalisation had always been pushed into my sub-conscious, and it hurt me for years thereafter. As I relate my life, I think it best to deal with it once and for all, so I may heal inside. The facts are that Abram went on for the priesthood in the Lutheran Church after finishing school and he became a powerful preacher. Quite recently he was ordained bishop of the Reformed Lutheran Church. It has congregations throughout South Africa, Botswana and Lesotho.

A few kilometres from Polonia lay a train station, Dewildt. There were adults working in Pretoria who boarded the six o' clock train and returned home in the eight o' clock train in the evening. Those going to Brits would catch the eleven o' clock train and return at three o' clock. There were also a few shops at Dewildt The village included an Indian shop, an Afrikaner shop where one of my uncle's worked, a Jewish business, a butchery, a post office, a police station, a clinic, and a garage but not of the present scale or standards. After school we always went to Dewildt on errands for our parents.

Much of Polonia's economy depended on the making of clay pots, which would then be sold in Pretoria and Brits. At times, women took loads of clay pots on ox-wagons, and stayed in places like Krugersdorp for six months on end selling their wares. They would come back with substantial sums of money. People also went to these towns occasionally to sell grapes, peaches, oranges and tomatoes.

Clay pots were made from a special red clay soil, which was found in the mountain at Mmakau. My paternal grandmother always told us how dangerous the place was where the soil was dug. There was one big rock, which projected beyond the others. It was under that rock that the special clay for making the pots was found.

The soil was mixed with water. Pots of different sizes and shapes would be moulded. To smooth them we used the rib of a cow with its graceful, natural curves. Then the pots were left to partially dry before being scraped inside to give a good finish. Next, parts of a broken calabash were dipped into wood ash. The outer rims of the pots would then be decorated with zigzag lines. When they were completely dry we used handfuls of morupetso, a kind of clay which was usually either black or red.

Girls my age did this job. We mixed the morupetso with water, blended it, and with a piece of cloth we coloured the pot and left it to dry out. We used a rounded stone to smooth the surface until it shone, and then polished it with a rag. The pots were now ready to be baked. Baking was done outside with fire fuelled by cow dung. Sheets of iron were put round the fire with pots placed between the burning clods of dung. When they had baked satisfactorily, they were taken out to cool before dusted and then packed away.

At my grandparents' house there was a special room where these pots were packed and stored. Even after filling the ox-wagon for the Krugersdorp market there would still be many left. When grandma returned from Krugersdorp, all those who helped with the decoration of her pots would be invited to the house for tea and bread. Grandma used some of the money she acquired this way to buy a farm, of which we are beneficiaries today.

Grandpa and grandma would leave Polonia at intervals during the year to go to Rankotea, a place where they reared cattle and cultivated crops. After harvest grandma would return with bags of maize and corn. This also was a farm, which grandpa, his younger brother and others bought. Today, platinum mines underlie this farm, and the family is receiving their royalties shared among the entire six households, comprising all my father's siblings. Unfortunately, because of the number of beneficiaries, with each household consisting of about six, little remains for other families.

During one of grandma's absences from Polonia, my paternal cousin who was ten years older than me started selling the pots in Pretoria on Saturdays. She would come back with money, which she used with her friends to buy good food for Sundays. This business went on until the stock of clay pots was exhausted. Grandma nearly fainted when she realized how the fruits of her hard work had been squandered. She asked neighbours if they had seen the ox-wagon that carried off her pots. The response was, "You have a two-legged ox-wagon in your household which has been partying on your property!" When my cousin was asked to account for the money she caused even greater offence by mentioning a farm that grandma had bought called 'Mankhekhetha.' The cousin retorted: "It was I who bought Mankhekhetha!" This was grandma's pride and joy because she had worked hard to buy it herself.

Grandpa, did not easily tolerate defiance, especially from a child. When sjamboking a culprit, he used the same whip as when driving his inspanned oxen. When he was told about what my cousin had done, he took her into a room, locked the door and sjamboked her so hard that grandma had to plead for her. The cousin was made to repay with every penny that she had in her possession. After this incident my cousin soon left Polonia to find a job in Johannesburg. She had reached only Standard Five.

After some years, she assisted her younger sister who ended up being a nurses' tutor at Baragwanath Hospital, known as Chris Hani Hospital today.

*Maggie, seated first row, second from right,*
*Mmanotshe Moduane Secondary School Debating Team*

# Rainy Days

◆

When it rained, we kids were encouraged to jump in the rain and say, *Sa ntlapulele! ke tla gôla leng (neng), ba bangwe ba godile! Rain, rain, when will I grow up like the others growing up!* Perhaps this is the reason that rain never hindered us from going on errands or carrying out household chores.

On rainy days, only children coming from beyond the village would be late for school. The reason for this is that they had to cross rivers which would be swollen and fast flowing on such days. I cannot remember ever having missed school because of rain as my childhood was spent within reasonable walking distance from school. Even if we did get soaked there was a wood fire waiting for us at home, and after drying out we would be so warm we would even venture outside to play in the rain.

In autumn when the crops were still fresh in the fields, we would be sent to the fields to harvest green mieles for cooking. Unlike today, there were no raincoats; we used empty sacks to cover our heads that covered our backs but not our fronts. As the sack became wet it would become heavier and heavier.

The interesting thing is that we seldom caught colds or flu. Today when children get wet they seem to catch a cold immediately and are also prone to flu. What has gone wrong with our bodies? We discourage children from playing in the rain, yet we buy them raincoats and umbrellas.

A bonus for children was that when it rained there was no need to fetch water as rainwater from the roofs was captured in drums. The houses at Moiletsane had flat zinc roofs, and we had water in abundance for bathing, washing and drinking. People preferred rain-water for laundry as it is soft it washes clothes far better than water from the well. At Polonia, however, we children were not as lucky, as the house roofs were thatched, and we still had to collect water, even in the rain.

In my childhood public transport was rare. Where I lived taxis and buses were non-existent and so we often walked very long distances in the rain. We thought we were lucky if we could ride on a donkey or in an ox cart: indeed, we considered such transport a luxury.

*My eldest sister Suzan.*

# Confirmation And Confusion

◆

I was 15 years old when I passed Standard Six, which is the present Grade Eight. That should have been the year to start confirmation classes. Unfortunately, I did not start, unlike my peer group back home.

The following year I was admitted to the Mmanotshe Moduane Secondary School, also known as Hebron Secondary School, where I started Standard Seven, then known as Form One.

My parents made an agreement with the missionary at home that I be allowed to attend confirmation class while still at secondary school. That way, I could be confirmed at home, together with my peer group.

When I got to Hebron, I immediately reported to the local missionary who had no problem with my request because I was already at secondary school level. But there was another problem. I was being ostracised by the confirmation class! The missionary had announced that I came from the Polonia congregation and though I was a year younger than the group there, he was ready to accept me for the sake of my peer group back home.

The difference here was that we attended confirmation classes once a week - on Friday afternoons, so the Hebron candidates had not covered as much as the Polonia candidates. This Friday afternoon arrangement was made to accommodate secondary school students. Pupils at primary schools, however, attended classes throughout the week.

Arriving at secondary school, I was compelled to join the debating team. I soon gained confidence and worked very hard to become a good speaker.

My membership of the debating team led to another glitch. Debates took place on Friday afternoons when I should have been attending confirmation class. I reported this to the missionary who did not seem to have a problem at all.

From my first days at Hebron I excelled and my subject teachers were quick to affirm me as their best student. I had come to Hebron because of the poverty of my family. I had wanted to go to Kilnerton Institution where I would do mathematics and be able to do Matric after the Junior Certificate.

Behrens, was at Bethel Training College; and Midah, was at a Catholic boarding school in Vleikop, called Notre Dame Secondary School. But here was I at Mmanotshe Moduane Secondary School.

Mathematics was not offered in our school, only arithmetic. My arithmetic teacher, Mr. Dammie, also complained. He truly wanted me to study maths. But what could I do because my parents were too poor to afford a better education for me? Here the fees were reasonable. We stayed in hostels but we provided our own meals. In time, turning necessity into a virtue, I accepted the situation.

At the end of that year, 1955, I did so well that I was advanced to Form Three, skipping Form Two altogether.

Back home I was faced with a confirmation test before I could be confirmed. When I got home, the other confirmants had all been already tested. There were only two of us, myself and a colleague -a boy who was at Kilnerton Institution. We were going to be tested alone.

Reverend Hans Dehnke, the Lutheran minister at Hebron, proved himself a very progressive educationist and pastor. He played down the value of rote learning, while here at home we had to recite the Catechism word for word. This I could no longer do. I tried the method we used at Hebron but this did not satisfy the impatient Rev Warneke, who was commonly known as: the Missionary!

Word had already spread that I had skipped a class, which meant that I was already too advanced for all my peers. But the Missionary was not impressed by that.

He ruled that I was not to be confirmed with the others, and would have to repeat the confirmation class the following year. This was a blow for my parents. My father tried to speak up on my behalf but Warneke replied, "Your daughter is very proud. She puts earthly things first and heavenly matters last. How could she fail a confirmation test when she was able to skip a class at school?"

At about midnight before Confirmation, one church council member knocked at my parents' door. He had brought news that finally the missionary had relented; yes I could be confirmed with my peers in the morning! Even this news did not bring any relief to my family. We felt insulted beyond words.

The following day it was raining cats and dogs. I prepared myself together with my parents to go to church. At last I was going to be confirmed; but instead of sentiments of joy, we felt like we were going to the funeral of a loved one.

The confirmation ceremony is usually long. I cannot remember fully and clearly all the details of the proceedings. I do not retain the memories of this big occasion, as others do. When the service ended it was still raining very hard. The confirmants routinely moved to the minister's house with their parents to receive their blessings. It is the custom in the Lutheran Church to be awarded blessings, which are lines of texts from the Bible. These texts are usually written during the course of the year. My personal crisis could therefore not have influenced my blessing. These blessings are supposed to be beacons guiding you through life's tough experiences.

All this while the rain had continued to pelt down and the soil at Polonia was red and sandy, with the water having already cut deep furrows. The Reverend started bestowing certificates of blessings on us confirmants. When it was my turn, whether by mistake, through anger or disgust, my certificate fell on the red, sandy soil and the man remained silent. No explanation, excuse, apology, he betrayed no emotion at all. He went on as if nothing untoward had happened. I was completely confused, even shocked, but in light of the events of the previous day, I kept my composure. This incident further disturbed my parents. I felt for them more than I did for myself.

I still feel today as I felt then. I had done nothing wrong to deserve such treatment. My peers came to my home urging me to join their parties. They understood my predicament and expressed their deep concern for my humiliation.

I picked up the soiled parchment. My blessing read, "Do not be afraid for I bring you good tidings which will be a joy to you and to all people."

These events affected my attitude towards the Missionary and towards the Lutheran Church in general. I have tried very hard to fight against this negative attitude. Because of the religious atmosphere in which I was raised, I have never ceased to talk to God even though I felt my church had let me down. I knew that one day I would find a religious home. After much searching I found this home at the age of forty. I converted to the Catholic Church and have never, ever regretted this change, or looked back. Father Don Campbell received me into the church, and afterwards, in 1979, Brother Gregory Staunton guided me through the catholic catechism.

*From left to right Reabetswe, Lebone and Masego grandchildren.*

*My father, Daniel with my two younger brothers - Lazarus and Abram*

# Part Two
# Culture
# And Tradition

# Tales Of Polonia

◆

There were stories that grandparents related to us when we were kids. There were also beliefs which we were expected to respect at all times without asking why.

One story that grandma at Polonia loved was an event during the Anglo-Boer War, now called the South African War.

Polonia was situated on a curve on the main road from Hartbeespoort Dam to DeWildt. The Boer fugitives moved at night and were desperate. At Polonia they'd see the lights and come into the village.

Separate from the main house there were huts outside which were used as kitchens and food stores. The security system was elementary: sometimes a string fastened to a nail, or a wooden latch. Dogs were the main threat; there was no theft in those days.

These fugitives apparently discovered their way to the huts and helped themselves to the provisions. Grandma complained one day that one of her children cried a lot during the night. Next night the paraffin lamp was therefore left alight because of the baby's restlessness. In due course they heard a knock at the door. There were several people, including women and children, waiting for that door to open. One of them exclaimed, Eina! Maak asseblief die deur oop. (Ouch! Please open the door).

Instinctively the child stopped crying. There was silence in the house and the lamp was put out. The door was left closed. The fugitives moved off.

Other stories related how as the Boer fugitives passed Polonia at night they would steal and kill pigs and chickens. At Polonia there were no goats, sheep or cattle. People reared only pigs and chicken.

Another story was the shortage of food that resulted from World War 2, the "Nazi wars", as we called them. People had to eat maize meal, which was mixed with anything you could think of even wood chips. One of my mother's cousins, Edward Motlhamme, nicknamed Iti, had been drafted into the South African army.

He must have travelled with the Allies as far north as Egypt. He related how a hail of bullets would sometimes fly above them like rain. He did not know how he survived, and believed he would never die having survived the dangers of war. But die he did, in the new Moiletswana, in about 1966.

The war had taken its toll on most of these veterans physically, emotionally, and psychologically. Their behaviour was not normal and some would dress up in their military uniforms and march up and down the streets as if preparing for action tomorrow. Nobody cared to counsel them but was there such a service as counselling available those days? When demobilized these soldiers had returned to their villages in South Africa. For their years in military service they were awarded bicycles, while their white counterparts were given farms.

There were lots of superstitions. When I went to fetch wood with grandma, she would warn me against certain types of trees; these I had to avoid. She'd be angry with me if I dared ask, "Why grandma?" I had to conform without asking why. We girls were not allowed into the cattle kraal. The belief was that the pregnant cows would bear stillborn calves. We were not allowed to eat while standing, as this would bring on future problems. If a boy ate from the pot he would develop breasts! If a woman was sweeping and you stood in her way, you'd find it difficult to get married.

A host of superstitions related to marriage. The bride preparing for marriage was not supposed to sample the home-brewed beer when it was still at the cooking stage. She was not supposed to eat cakes that were baked for her wedding because this would result in heavy rain which would spoil her big day. In case it rained during a wedding feast or threatened rain, there were branches of a certain tree, which when thrown on the fire, would stop the rain. Sometimes rough salt was poured on the flames for the same purpose. Such beliefs clearly reflect a pre-scientific culture

Different parts of the ox were assigned to guests according to how they were related to the groom/bride or the deceased. The head belonged to the maternal uncle. The ribs from each side were divided between the maternal and paternal aunts - people did not just come to fetch the meat. Guests had to prepare food that would be served during the wedding.

In the case of funeral celebrations the uncle would pay a condolence before taking the head. Some guests preferred to have the head cooked at the home of the deceased and consumed there instead of taking it home. The uncle and his spouse were also responsible for shaving the heads of their nieces and nephews after the funeral of their parents. I have noticed that in some cultures this function is given to paternal aunts.

Kidneys were not supposed to be eaten by younger women who had not as yet given birth. This kind of meat was feared to produce adverse effects on child-bearing. Kidneys were therefore reserved for older women and men. Pregnant women were not to eat eggs, as it was believed they would induce childbirth difficulties. But those eggs that were abandoned by the hen when the chicks were hatched were given to us children. We would boil the eggs, sometimes finding a chicken inside. We just removed it and ate the remainder even though it was black in colour.

It was taboo to request salt after sunset. If you did so, you had to pour out a few grains of it on your way out at the exit. The salt leaving your house after sunset was believed to be a bad omen.

Even the local Indian shops, I remember, refused to sell salt after sunset! After the birth of a baby, outsiders were not allowed inside. A log was placed across the entrance of the house, to remind people they were not welcome. It was also the case when there was someone very ill in the family. If visitors dropped in as usual, it was feared they would make the sick person develop complications. Visitors or even members of the family were forbidden to enter a new baby's room or that of a sick person, when returning from funerals, or from any large gathering of any sort.

Some of these superstitious practices are still in use. I was amazed this year when making a courtesy visit to a young teacher, to witness the log being used. When I registered my surprise that this custom was still in use in 2005, the young mother explained that it was to ward off irresponsible teenagers from visiting her new-born and contaminating him. But then the log was fulfilling a very useful purpose: keeping unwelcome visitors out. So was it a case of superstition at all?

The umbilical cord of the newly born baby was buried in the yard. This united the baby, the home and the environment (community of the child). People are always proud to say my umbilical cord was buried here, Kalana ya me e wetse fa. It affirms the speaker as a true child of the soil.

Old people had ways of healing infants' ailments. There were always experts in the community who could cure children's ills. The most commonly used herbs were lengana and ditantanyane. I still remember that for measles we were kept in a dark room, we ate salt-less food, and drank specially prepared lengana.

Wounds, including burns, were cleaned with salt water. For boils there was a wild plant with thick leaves which were warmed up. The outside of the leaf was removed. The warm leaf was placed on the boil or growth, which was then bandaged. This treatment was repeated daily resulting in the boil opening up and emitting the puss. The infected part was washed daily with salt water until it healed. This plant also served as a disinfectant. Even today at funerals when mourners return from graveyards, they wash their hands in water containing this herb.

When we developed mumps, we were advised to wake up very early in the morning before anyone else, and before sunrise. We would then go to a large empty clay pot, bend with your head inside, saying, mauwe-uwe, mauwe-uwe, boela nkgong. "Mumps, mumps, return to the clay pot." This belief helped us to recover.

At Polonia, grandma regularly saw ghosts but was never scared. We asked her why they did not scare her. Her answer was "Why should they? I've not killed anyone!" She often went to the banks of the Crocodile River where she collected the reeds for making floor mats. Sometimes she would work up to very late at night. In those days people were not afraid of each other. Today we fear people who have become criminals  even our family members who have turned to crime. That time, ghosts were the only things we feared at night.

On one of grandma's visits to the Crocodile River for reeds my cousin Mmampepu, accompanied her. As usual they worked until dark. On their way back, they saw this ghost playing tricks on them and making it difficult for them to find the right path home. It made a very bright light around them, and then it darkened again. This trick was repeated. Mmampepu also witnessed this and clutched grandma's skirt. Grandma was not sure that Mmampepu was aware of what was happening.

Pointing with a stick towards the light that was playing around, she asked Mmampepu, "Can you see it?" Mmampepu was both angry and frightened at the same time. She was angry because grandma was quite relaxed; she was frightened because she was in the scary presence of a ghost. She wondered what else they were going to witness that night! The ghost made it so difficult for them to move along, that they sat under a tree and spent the night there.

We were always advised to sit when not doing anything. Boys and men would never enter the house with their hats on; this would be a sign of disrespect. When talking to elderly people, boys held their hats in their hand. Young people stood up when an elderly person talked to them. But these polite codes of behaviour were not universal, however. As principal of Tshukudu High School, I discovered a different form of respect from my scholars who had fled urban areas because of the Soweto riots. They would come to my office and would never speak until they had seated themselves on a chair. I soon realised that this was not defiance, but another form of respect. Of course, I did my research about this style of behaviour and I was surprised to discover standing up would be tantamount to a challenge to fight!

Children of our ages greeted every adult they met. Any adult could send them on errands. Not so today, because of changes in our societal values. Crime also contributed to these changes. Children are abducted, sexually abused, kept as sex slaves, or even murdered. There is a general mistrust even of adults we know quite well.

There were other stories that we were told as kids while in Polonia. People were warned against passing by the hill at Makau at noon. It was believed that that was the time when ancestors were busy there. Passers by who deliberately ignored this warning came with descriptions of people talking as if a community gathering was in progress. But all was invisible. They heard herdsmen calling their cattle, the stumping of corn in wooden blocks, children crying, others playing. However, no witness ever claimed to have seen anything. There were only the familiar sounds of normal village life. Many people were thus scared to even venture near the mill at noon. Today the same hill is said to hold a lot of granite and work is proceeding to mine it. It was called Thaba ya Badimo, "The Ancestors' Hill".

Belief in big serpents that occupied dams and rivers curtailed the social life of communities. People were warned against disturbing these dangerous snakes or they would experience storms, or other natural disasters. Hurricanes were caused by the serpent's movement from one river that was drying up, to another with more water. On its journey it would cause untold havoc.

We knew whose daughter grandma was. Whenever she was puzzled by something she would invoke her father's name; "Ka Ra-Mpelegeng-wa-Ngwajipane". So we knew her father was Ra-Mpelegeng. One of her siblings was Mpelegeng; hence, Ra-Mpelegeng, meaning, father of Mpelegeng. By all accounts her family lived at a place called Kudube. The community there had not been converted to Christianity. She must have been a beautiful person during her youthful days. Her name was Maria and her ancestral name, Mmampee. She had been known as Maria, the Beautiful. Apparently she shared the name with other women; otherwise the community called her Mmantlhwa's spouse. Grandpa's traditional name was Mmantlhwa.

Grandma was not only light in complexion with black lips; she was not only beautiful, she was also neat. Before she left her house to draw water or do anything outside her home, she would wash and change to clean clothes. When neighbours saw her, they would enquire if it was Sunday. They were not aware of the days of the week. They only knew that Christians looked neat on Sunday when they attended church services. They always associated cleanliness with Sunday. It also seems that the community did not speak the same dialect as grandma and her family. One day when she had washed and changed to clean clothes, somebody approached her. She looked at grandma up and down remarking, "Coco-codii! Beautiful from head to toe!"

*Solomon husband.*

# Stories About Grandma

◆

G randma at Polonia received all and sundry in her household. Some of her stories were about the different people she befriended. We grew up at the time when different ethnic groups had little respect for one another. There were many Shangaan (Tsonga) kids who schooled with us. There were Shangaan friends who visited her from time to time. They bought some of her handicrafts or they came to buy a pig. Grandma also reared pigs for sale. Sometimes she slaughtered a pig, sold the meat and kept the fat to make soap. We used homemade soap most of the time. To make soap the fat was cooked in big pots and then they added caustic soda. This soda was very poisonous, and we were always ordered to stay away from it. Once cooked, it was dried and then cut into manageable sizes, and kept aside to dry out more.

When the Shagaans entered the village, children would follow them until they reached their destination. When they entered our home, the onlookers would peep curiously over the walls watching as they were engaged in conversation with grandma. They would then run back to call others telling them, "Come and see Ma-Shagaan at Abram's home!" They did this all the time when these visitors came to our house. At school the following day they would then tease us, in a mild form of xenophobia, about the kind of visitors grandma entertained. When it was dark, grandma would rather have them sleep over than allow them to be humiliated or even injured in the darkness of the night. We called them dichomi tsa koko, grandma's friends. They referred to grandma as mokhotse, meaning friend.

One day, in one of her stories, grandma had refused to sell her pig. When it was time to sleep she offered her friend a pillow. Little did grandma realise that her friend was angry. When the pillow came, her friend said Mokhekhole, o ntse o re mdamelo, mdamelo kana ka mdamela nene? "Old lady you keep on offering me a pillow. When did you ever see me using it?" This remark disturbed grandma, because her intention had not been to cause conflict. She had other plans for the pig. Early the following day, while Koko was still in bed, her friend departed and never even bothered to say goodbye. This was the price she paid for her kindness. But still, she would continue welcoming this ungrateful friend, when she returned.

Grandma and mom got on very well together. Actually grandma was very protective towards mom and us. We meant the world to her. She was just loving and very simple and easy to get on with. I never heard or saw grandma get angry with her daughters-in-law like I was told other old women did. When one of them treated her badly or with disrespect, she would never complain or report the incident to others. She loved peace and lived in harmony with all around her. But people have the tendency of taking advantage of each other's kindnesses. It happened with grandma and my mom. Even when we came home crying having been rough-handled or insulted by someone outside, I have never seen them do what others did: go to the street and shout! They always handled these problems with the calmness and the dignity they deserved. This behaviour of the two women in our lives has influenced us even to this day. None of us would ever be found shouting in the street no matter how hurt we might feel. Such behaviour always frightens us. It is something we are never able to handle even when we are the victims of the shouting. However, I'm different from my siblings. In meetings, I am able to put my point across. I can state very strongly what I like or dislike and what is right or wrong, under the protection of the chair of course.

While we stayed with grandma at Polonia, several of her relations would come to stay with us. Some came to do Standard Six at Polonia School as their home schools ended at Standard Five. One particular relative, a man, was the same peer group as my brother Behrens. He came from where grandpa had bought a farm. He was a handsome young man, very light in complexion, similar to a Coloured person. You could see this from his curly hair and blue eyes. Again the children of Polonia would peep over the high walls and shout to the others, Tlaang lo bone lekgoa kwa gaabo Abram, "Come and see a white person at Abram's home." He, Behrens and our cousin, passed Standard Six together. They all proceeded to Bethel Training School. However, he left school early and found a good job in Johannesburg. Having classified as Coloured, he received good wages. Soon he had opened a number of businesses and was counted among the wealthiest men in and around Mmakau. While grandma was still alive, he visited us regularly. But, afterwards when grandma had died, we never saw him again. However, when his own turn came, we all attended his funeral.

Then there was an old lady, Mrs. Kungwane, who also came to stay with us. She was the wife of grandma's brother. She came to Polonia for Catechism classes, so that she could be baptised and confirmed before marriage. The problem was she was illiterate. Before she could learn Catechism, she went through a crash course in reading and writing. We were also asked to assist her but it wasn't easy. However, we persevered and she too committed herself with patience to our teaching. We were just kids ourselves. Abram and I wrote on the slate and asked her to read the letters. Sometimes she would be amused saying some of the letters like g, d and a, had tails! On certain occasions she would be angry, thinking that we were not teaching her the right things. Having completed the course, she was baptised and confirmed. The marriage was blessed in church.

As I said grandma was generous and very accommodating. People did not request to stay with her. They just pitched up, and stayed on as if it was their right.

During those days relatives would visit for days without any prior notice. That is why we have the Setswana proverb, moeng goroga re je: "When a visitor comes there'll be plenty to eat".

A chicken, a goat or sheep would be prepared for the visitor. When it was time for him/her to leave, the same procedure was carried out. He would be given a portion of the meat to take home. Dumplings, fat cakes or bread were other parting gifts. If it was autumn he would take green mielies and other products from the fields.

My dad was very strict and sometimes went over the limit scolding and beating us. Grandma would not listen to all that without intervening. That is why whenever dad was angry with us; he first had to check where grandma was. He always complained that grandma was spoiling us. But she was just a good person. It taught us so much. The legacy she left behind was the importance of education. She always saved the meagre pension fund she received to assist us at school. When she had sold her clay pots and handicrafts, she always spared something for our education. She was ready to share whatever she had with us no matter how little.

One of my most painful childhood memories concerns Lazarus. My sister, Midah and I, had accompanied mom to Rankotea where grandpa kept his livestock. Lazarus was a toddler. While mother was busy with the chores inside the hut, we played outside. In our play we became careless and reckless and put our younger brother in a sack. We were about to close it when mother suddenly appeared. She was very upset, and pointed out to us the danger of suffocation. Only then did we realise the stupidity of our game. This gave me some troubled afterthoughts. What if Lazarus had really died because of our silly game?

*Maggie with a group of Wayfarers at Tapos Primary School.*

# What's In A Name?

◆

Family names tend to be derived from those who came before us, our ancestors. Certain names are predominant and run from generation to generation in my mother's family; the name Lazarus is very common. Lazarus is my maternal grandfather. My younger brother is Lazarus. One of my aunt's sons also bears that name. In other households of my mother's family, you'll always find one named Lazarus. Sometimes they shorten it to Lasi. My mother's maternal uncle was Behrens. My eldest brother was also named Behrens. The old man, Behrens, was very tough and stubborn and never surrendered easily when committed to a cause he believed in. He was also an independent thinker.

Sometimes in our culture we say, Leina le ya borellong, meaning: "You have acquired the traits of the person you've been named after". My brother Behrens was the same as the old Behrens he was named after, and so was my uncle of the same name.

I was named after my paternal grandmother, a very gentle and forgiving old lady. Her traditional name was Mampee. This name was never used at all for me. Grandma alone used this name, and she always referred to me as her namesake. We had a lot in common. She was a great storyteller, and as a result, we spent a lot of time together, enjoying her never-ending narratives which left me either laughing or mesmerized. She greatly prized peace and quietness. Other children in our extended family also loved her and she received numerous presents from them. She was particular about what she wore. She would instruct one to bring a skirt that was bought by so-and-so, or a blouse by so-and-so. So too with the headscarves and shoes.

I was also named after an old lady who lived in the back of our house. She was called Ma-Gideon, meaning mother of Gideon. My sister Midah apparently could not pronounce this name when she played with me when I was a baby. Instead of Ma-Gideon, she said Machinto. I am therefore, generally known as Machinto by all those close to me and all who know me well; and those I played with and attended primary school with. Immediately a person says this name, I jump with excitement because I realise she/he knows me intimately. The name is very close to my heart. Interestingly enough, none of my official documents carry this name.

On the other hand, when I was young, I could not pronounce my younger brother's name- Lazarus. I called him Latu, instead of Lasi. This name has also become accepted in family circles, and among all those who know him well.

My sister Midah was named after our eldest paternal aunt. Very few people understood our aunt. She complained, found fault with everything and everybody, and could always remember more wrongs than rights about people. She was also very talkative and would repeat the same event over and over again. Sometimes as she related an incident, she would ramble on to a second or even third event, and thus lose track of the original. Nevertheless, she related her experiences with a passion, whether anyone listened or not!

We always avoided conversations with her because she would hold you there, expecting you to just listen and say nothing. She had the weakness of regarding herself as being right all the time. There was no way you could convince her otherwise.

I realised when I grew up that I had excellent listening skills. From secondary school onwards, I was always chosen as secretary of school organisations. They were sure to have their minutes up to date. I spoke very little, but could record the discussions as they were.

Secretaries today act differently; they do more talking than taking down notes. In our days, secretaries did very little talking, except when they wanted to verify a point with the meeting, before recording it in writing.

My maternal grandma was Anna, and her other name, which was commonly used was Ma-Fini, mother of Fini. My aunt's name was Ephenia, shortened to Fini. This is also a commonly used name in our family circles.

Mothers are usually named after their first-born children. My paternal grandma was known as Ma-Abbiot; my father's eldest brother being Abbiot. The reason my grandma at Moiletswane was known as Ma-Fini and not Ma-Martha, while Fini was the second child was that when the family arrived from Monyamane, my mother was already six years old, and so Fini was the first child born at Moiletswane. And so, Fini became a commonly known name of my mother's siblings.

My youngest brother's name, Abram, is common among our paternal households. Our eldest sister's name Suzan is a very popular choice from our maternal side. Martha, a name translated as Maadimo, frequently turns up. We also have several examples of David Talo, derived from our only surviving maternal uncle.

The trend today is to give children names from sources other than tradition. Some names derive from Bible passages and try to encourage children positively. They also reflect the family's relationships with God, and their view of life. Other names are derived from incidents in people's lives. My brother, Abram, named his first-born Boitshoko, (Patience). The second-born is Tshegofalang (Be-blessed); and the third is Solofelang (Have Hope).

We also come across names such as Tshepo (Hope); Keamogetse (I-have-received); Keamogetswe (I-am-welcome); Neo or Mpho (Gift); Kgomotso (Comfort); Goitsemang (Who- knows); Kealeboga (Thank-you-God); Lebogang (Say-thanks-to- God); and Kelebogile (I-am-thankful). The name Kgomotso is always given to a child born immediately after a family bereavement. And so the child is regarded as God's way of comforting the family.

These names carry profoundly religious connotations. Tshepo expresses hope in Modimo, Neo, Mpho, Kealeboga, and Kelebogile all express thanks to Modimo, the giver of life.

Ancestral names are beginning to be ignored, because of the belief that you not only inherit the name, but also the personality of your namesake. I don't know of anybody who would dream of naming a child Hitler, or Jonas Savimbi, or Idi Amin!

Traditionally a child who inherited a name was given the same respect and status that would be given the elder namesake. Grandma at Moiletswane treated my younger brother, Lazarus; with the same respect she gave grandpa. Lazarus was treated differently from all of us; always receiving the best. Not only did grandma honour Lazarus, but also my aunts and uncles gave him that respect.

grandma lovingly called him 'Oula', meaning old man Lazarus. My aunts and uncles referred to him as 'monna-mogolo', meaning old man. Lazarus was offered the best place next to the fire when it was cold. The best food was always left for him. In a way, he was respected at Moiletswane. To date, he and the other Lazarus are favourites among our maternal relatives.

At Polonia my paternal grandma gave me the same respect, having been named after her. We were like peers. I would sit on her lap while she related her stories to me. Abram our youngest brother was similarly honoured at Polonia. He was named after one of grandma's brothers. Thus he was respected as uncle to my dad and his siblings. While we sat with grandma, we also asked her numerous questions. One question which Abram asked and which grandma dodged was, if like we were told at school that God created all and us and everything else, who created God? Today Abram is a pastor of the Lutheran church. I wonder whether he will be able to answer this question!

*Maggie at Nairobi game reserve.*

# Clashing Of Traditions

---◆---

When the Lutheran Missionaries settled at Polonia, the Roman Catholic Missionaries came to settle at Mmakau, the site of the chief's kgotla. The Catholics were soon followed by the Anglicans. Other Lutheran Missionaries also settled in the vicinity of Mmakau, at Hebron and other Bakwena regions.

In no time, the Catholics and Anglicans at Mmakau were sending children to higher institutions to get degrees, while the Lutherans at Polonia encouraged people to go only as far as teacher training college, e.g. their own college at Bethel. A few women students went for nursing. Careers in social work were as yet unheard of in those days.

At Hebron the jaar system still prevailed. After Confirmation children were encouraged to leave school and work on the neighbouring farms for a jaar, an Afrikaans term 'jaar' meaning a year. On the day of the Confirmation, local boers, the Afrikaner farmers, arrived with trucks, tractors and carts to take the confirmants to work at their farms. At the end of the year, the boy would be awarded a cow, and the girl a dining room suite. In the economic conditions of the 1940s these rewards were accepted by many as fair compensation for a year's work. Others took a different view.

Added to this jara practice, was the fact that the Lutheran children were not encouraged to study as much as the Catholics and Anglicans. As a result, local people started boycotting the church. The anger reached such a pitch that the old Lutheran church building was burnt down. Two conflicting groups emerged within the community: The one group viewed the whole jara system as a form of social exploitation; the other saw nothing wrong in the deal between the Lutheran missionaries and the local boers.

When I started secondary school at Hebron in 1955 some of the ring-leaders of this church boycott and burning were still around. There was one old man who was in the parent-representative body of the school, who in my view was very learned and brilliant. We always looked forward to school re-openings and important functions when he would be addressing us. He would list all the highly educated men and women he knew, and encouraged us to emulate them. Surprisingly enough, he also emphasised women elites so as to motivate us girls. He had named his children after Zulu leaders and warriors. I can remember that one of his sons was Shaka, and another Mzilikazi. Those old men were the democrats of yesteryear.

Missionaries of different denominations had differing approaches to evangelization when they settled among black communities. Most missionaries attended to the full Christian and human development of their adherents. Thus the Anglicans ran a secondary school called St. Peter's, which carried students all the way to Matric and was among the best in the country.

The Methodists had Kilnerton, which was also of a high standard. The Catholics ran several schools but separated boys from girls. Famous Catholic institutions included St. Thomas, Pax College, Notre Dame and St. Mary's. All missionary schools set very high standards in education, with the possible exception of the Lutherans.

The Lutherans seemed to take a somewhat different approach to evangelization. Unlike the other missionaries, they emphasized religious formation through catechism, Bible and worship, above and beyond human development. Lutheran primary schools generally did not motivate students to study beyond Confirmation. Nor did they provide secondary schools. Their theology seemed to draw a very clear line between the spiritual and the temporal, between the heavenly and the mundane. "Seek first the Kingdom of God," was oft repeated by our pastors in Polonia, even as their more "worldly" Anglican, Methodist and Catholic brothers were celebrating ever better matric results!

Thus it was only very late in life that students from Lutheran institutions could access tertiary education. An example is found in the person of Solomon Malao of Bethanie who was the first in the area to graduate with a BA from

UNISA. Other exceptions were Otto Maboe and his wife who were Hebron's first BA graduates. I was there to participate in the celebrations. Of course, Mrs Maboe broke new ground as the first woman in the region to graduate.

Another source of misunderstanding between missionaries and their black adherents arose over the matter of names. New names were given to new Christians, usually on the occasion of their baptism. Re-born in the baptismal waters, the person was christened and inducted among the Communion of Saints, the saved badimo. Hence, the church tradition of bestowing the name of saints on their new members.

But this should not excuse those missionaries who failed to appreciate the cultural richness of our African names; names such as Mmapula, Rapula that are female and male names, respectively, for: "One born on a rainy day". Dikeledi means "tears". Tshepo is "hope". Basetsana is the name given to a girl in an all-girl family. And Basimane, the name given to a boy in an all-boy family. Ignoring these African names, they imposed those of the Bible. Thus names such as Esther, Aaron, Moses, Jacob, Bethseba, Sarah, Solomon, and Susan are popular among us today, even if only as appendages which appear on our official documents.

The story goes that when children were introduced to Bible classes, they were queued, so that each one's name could be registered. Because the names they were given were new to these children, they would easily forget them. Sometimes a girl would mistakenly give the name of an older or younger sister. Or if a boy in front said Aaron, all those who followed would repeat the name!

I found a similar prejudice towards African names in the Catholic Church also. Here a major emphasis is placed on the names of Christian saints, whether dating from the 12 apostles and the early church, or from recent centuries. Popular among Catholic men are names such as Andrew, John, Peter, Thomas, Phillip, James, and Mathew. Popular names for women are also heavily influenced by the same source that is the apostles, thus giving us Andrea, Johanna, Petra...The names Agnes, Cecilia, Anastasia honour women martyrs from the early church. Topping the list of New Testament names are Mary, Anne, Elizabeth and Magdalene.

As blacks of course we welcome the names of newly canonised African saints like Lwanga and Bekitha. But whether sourced from Bible or church such names are much more than maina a sekgoa! They are truly universal.

Dates of birth and age posed another problem. People were given ages according to the assessment made by the missionary. Circumcision schools were put on hold. Polygamy was also discouraged. Where a man was married to two or more women, he was advised to marry one of them in a Christian way, and divorce the rest. Ancestral devotions and most forms of traditional healing were regarded as forms of paganism.

Little did people realise that they were made to throw away what they really were, and that they were left with nothing that could be called their own, nothing to be proud of as black people. Later in life they would regret they allowed this to happen.

Pupils who were fast learners of the Bible and Catechism were encouraged to become teachers. The Church and the school were inseparable. The early missionaries also taught people how to read and write their language. Those who passed Catechism classes had mastered basic literacy and numeracy also and therefore were qualified to find gainful employment in urban areas. Unlike other denominations such as Anglicans, Methodists and Catholics who came much later, the missionaries encouraged their members to learn other languages such as English, and were sent to higher institutions of learning to acquire better qualifications. These missionaries made funds available for their members to study.

When the missionaries arrived, they found that in times of drought people would naturally look to the kgosi, the chief, for rain. The kgosi and his kgotla would then summon the tribal traditional healer to prepare his medicines. A day would then be set aside for prayer to the ancestors. Young girls who were still virgins were called upon to gather at the kgotla early on the morning of the prayer day. Each was given a clay pot containing the mixture prepared by the traditional healer. They were to carry these vessels on their heads. They were instructed to go all over the veld, walking in single file while dipping a horsetail in the mixture and sprinkling the stuff on trees, shrubs and grass as they moved along. All the mixture had to be used up. The girls would take a different route on their way back to the kgotla. From here the elders, the kgosi and the traditional healer set out for the mountain, singing as one. There they pleaded with the ancestors through the kgosi and the traditional healer, to grant them pula, rain. From here they would return to the kgotla in silence. Branches of a tree called mosetlha which they carried would be piled at the kgotla. The ceremony climaxed with the burning of these branches. By late afternoon or evening heavy cumulus clouds would start forming, followed by showers of precious pula!

How much of this rain-making was strictly scientific, and how much was pure co-incidence? Was it science or plain nonsense? These questions seemed not to worry the chief and his medicine man that ascribed it all to the power of the badimo. That was their belief. But the missionaries were not at all convinced; no more than our modern meteorologists would be.

In their cold rationalist minds, religion with science amounted to superstition. And it was superstition that held people in bondage. Little wonder that after such a rain-inducing ceremony the kgosi found himself in trouble. If he persisted he could find himself excommunicated for performing an act contrary to Christianity.

The missionaries' message and methods clashed with the belief systems and religious practices of black people as well as their core cultural symbols. The power of such traditional leaders as dikgosi, elders and medicine men was being seriously challenged. These inevitably lost the loyalty of the tribe who witnessed a new order, and a new set of foreign symbols emerging before their eyes. Inevitably this clash of symbols left many - on both sides - somewhat confused, and the confusion persists in some measure to this day.

For far too long African beliefs and values have been assumed to be totally incompatible with the good news of the Gospel. However, today's theologians think differently. It seems to me that the task of 'enculturation' is urgent indeed!

I have known some missionaries, the rare few who could live comfortably with apartheid, who expressed a rather negative attitude towards educated black people. They seemed threatened when a black person pursued university studies and could express him or herself in fluent English. They referred to such individuals as lost, as betrayers; or worst of all, as communists. Communist was synonymous with satanic; a communist was assumed to be an atheist, and therefore was viewed as the devil incarnate.

During the early times of these missionaries, when two people wanted to get married, the intended marriage was announced in church for three consecutive Sundays. Anyone opposed to such a marriage was asked to speak up and say why, or thereafter remain silent. In all my life in this church I have never seen or heard anyone opposing an intended marriage, at least not publicly.

If before marriage the bride was pregnant or already had a child, the wedding was perceived as dishonourable. The bride in such circumstances was not supposed to wear a veil on the wedding day. That custom posed its own dangers. What about the brides who were in fact pregnant? Were they to publicly disgrace themselves? No wonder we heard whispered stories of abortions! Another painful aspect was seldom raised: The male partners, who were equally guilty, escaped scot-free. How come?

For many days before the pending marriage the girls of my age then, went to the groom's and bride's homes every evening to rehearse wedding songs and dances for the ceremony.

Marriages started with lobola being paid by the groom's family in the form of cows. Divorce was very rare and was perceived, according to the norms of the day, as a disgrace. For two to cohabitate was unheard of. If it happened, usually in towns where young people were employed as domestic servants, news would quickly reach home and people would raise eyebrows.

Custom required that the firstborn child after a marriage be born at the woman's home. These were occasions when the young woman was well looked after by her mother. She would stay indoors for a period of a month and only ventured out on the day her baby was baptised. Having been well catered for, she would appear even more beautiful than on her wedding day. First baptisms were occasions of great celebrations, minor disagreements about choice of names notwithstanding!

It was common for us local girls in those days to fetch plentiful supplies of water for the family of the newborn. We looked forward to sharing the delicacies usually prepared for the young mother. Sometimes a sheep, a goat or even an ox was slaughtered because she herself had to be well nourished if she was to nurse her infant properly.

I lived at a time when new mothers were well looked after. When my son Kennedy was born, I spent ten days in a nursing home. As I did not have anyone else to do the baby's washing, I had to do it myself. It was the same with Olivia, my second born. With Harold, my third born, it was even worse. I stayed for only three days in hospital but I was fortunate to have an elderly lady, a mother of my friend, who volunteered to look after the baby and myself for two weeks. I resumed work on the third week.

Harold was born during a mid-winter cold spell when I saw snow for the first time in my life. Actually I feared for the baby's health in hospital; his cot was right at an open window. But my fears were all ill-founded. Harold grew up to be the healthiest one of the family, and rarely consults a doctor. He is health conscious in what he eats and the way he conducts his life generally.

Kennedy and Olivia were born while we were employed at Bethel Training School. They were born at a German nursing home, not far from where we lived. They were baptised by Moruti Hans Dehnke, at the Bethel Lutheran Church - the same missionary who conducted Confirmation classes while I was a student at Hebron. He was the same pastor who married us in 1960.

Harold was born at Potchefstroom where we settled for a while after leaving Bethel. We left Potchefstroom before he was baptised. Moruti Dehnke had by coincidence also moved back to Hebron and he baptised Harold in the Lutheran church there.

*My self in Malawi.*

# An Unsung Hero And Heroine

---

◆

---

My mother was very ill on one of my last visits to her; she could not speak properly because of the pain. I informed her that I was appointed Chief Circuit Officer, She remarked feebly but with obvious satisfaction, Oh! Mandela o go file tiro? Oh! Popo o go file tiro? ("Has Mandela offered you a job? Has Popo offered you a job?").

In the depth of pain she experienced, she could only smile with excitement. She is the one who saw me suffer and struggle for the previous six hectic years. Can you imagine what I had gone through trying to cope with prisons, courts, and oncologists while at the same time looking after my grandchildren, and feeling guilty about the deteriorating condition of my mother? Of course, mother had suffered with me. Now she was departing this life without the chance to savour the fruits of my achievements.

After two weeks my mother died in hospital, having said goodbye to all her children, grandchildren and great-grandchildren with the blessing, Kagiso e nne le lona (Peace be with you!) I cried uncontrollably. But not everyone was crying. Some felt she had been released at last from her acute pain. They were unaware of why I cried so much. I had come home to restore my mother to her happiness after much grief. Now she had slipped away from my life. Just like that! I could not come to terms with my loss.

Mother was a strong-willed personality, and was a powerful hidden force who motivated me to persevere against all the odds. Hers was a hidden struggle while mine was open and public. She remains one of the many unsung heroines who helped to give birth to the new South Africa.

Remember she was the one who worked as a domestic servant in Johannesburg all her life to see us through our education. Surely she deserved happiness at the end of her life. She had struggled through asthma for years and now she had died of a tumour in her stomach. That was diagnosed when she was already too weak to be operated on.

She was 84 years of age when she died, having been born in the year of the birth of the Union of South Africa in 1910. My father had died 19 years earlier at the relatively young age of 58. That was before we were moved from Polonia to an area called Ramogodi.

The death of my father came with the birth of Ga-Rankuwa in 1965. He was working at a construction site as the township was being built. He met his accident when one of the earth-moving caterpillar vehicles accidentally drove over him, killing him instantly. He died at the time I had just arrived at Hebron and was employed in the male residence. At that time no-one thought of suing the construction company. How times have changed!

There was little opportunity for my mother to escape into mourning. The demands of family were too pressing. She had to pay fees for my younger brothers who were still at school. She stayed at home for only three months, and not for a year, as tradition demanded.

In 1990 while I was convalescing from mastectomy, our eldest brother Behrens also passed away. He was 57. My elder sister, Midah, is now 68 years old - a retired teacher. I am now, as of writing, 65 years of age, and also retired. Our younger brothers, Lazarus and Abram are aged 61 and 55, respectively.

My mother was an outstanding cook. Many of the recipes I use I learned from her. When I visited her at her workplace she made me help her in the kitchen, and thus I learned a great deal. Sometimes her employer would offer me a part-time job for holidays. This helped my mother to meet some of my expenses.

Mother was very religious. With her, every problem, sorrow or misfortune was God's way of making you understand and know Him. She never feared the unknown, unlike the majority of people around her. She taught us to pray. I cannot remember her ever exchanging angry words with anybody. She never took sides in a dispute. When as children we fought, she would just advise us to respect the older sister/brother; the older one would be advised to protect the younger sibling.

She was very devout. Sunday to her meant one thing, and one thing only - going to church. She was thus loved and respected by many, while others took advantage of her meekness. She loved education with a passion. She read without glasses even up to the end. She could read a newspaper and liked to relate what she read to others. She read the Bible daily.

Father was a pipe smoker. He used tobacco called Horse Shoe, which he sent us to buy at De Wildt from time to time. He smoked casually, even in bed. His presence was always felt because of the Horse Shoe aroma. During those days this tobacco was packed in small bags and when it was finished, my grandmother would wash the bags, using them as a purse, whenever she had sold large amounts of clay pots, or after receiving her pension.

My mother did not eat pork. It therefore followed that the rest of us would not eat it either. Only my father ate it. We could not prepare it to his liking and therefore he prepared it himself. He would make it so attractive, golden brown, but we did not like it.

*Neo grandson.*

# Part Three
# Death, Burial And The Ancestors

# First Experience Of Death And Burial Rites

◆

I first experienced bereavement in the family at the age of six when my paternal grandfather, Lazarus, died at Moiletswane. It was quite a confusing event, as we children did not understand what was going on. The family mourned. Relatives from near and far came to pay their respects. Church members in their uniform of yellow and white prayed with the family everyday until the burial.

As the women folk approached the house they carried on their heads maize meal and other items to be cooked for the occasion. The maize meal was taken and poured into bags. The family did not buy the meal for the occasion. These women got into single file as they approached the house, weeping. Their lamentation asked: "Lazarus, why do you leave the children?"

There were no mortuaries at the time. The dead were therefore kept for a few days before burial. I still remember that grandfather was buried on the very next day. The corpse was waked in a cool room, on a zinc bed, and covered with cloth. Men relatives at home made the coffin. It was shouldered by relatives to the cemetery unaided by any kind of vehicle.

The cooked meal was very simple - pap. Sometime it was sour porridge or both. An ox was slaughtered for the official funeral meal. I have never seen any vegetables served, or fancy items, except tea.

Before the funeral young women brought flowers, of the kind we usually saw growing in graveyards. They also brought wild plants, which they wove into funeral wreaths.

At Polonia again I experienced the deaths of my paternal aunt and some of her grandchildren. The procedure was almost the same. I have never seen the mourners going to church first. From the home of the deceased they proceeded straight to the graveyard, singing hymns as they filed along. We children were never part of these occasions. In fact, children of the bereaved family would be sent to a relative's house where they stayed until the event was over. Our food was sent there.

As the funeral procession filed through the streets, children would run indoors. Children were not allowed to witness any part of the bereavement. Burials took place on weekdays, and within daylight hours. In Polonia the school I attended was situated on the road to the graveyard. On funeral days, we would be kept inside until the procession had passed.

Funerals were viewed as occasions where people mourned their dead. No delicacies were expected therefore. Even the cooked meat was served without salt.

During those days we seldom witnessed deaths of young children. Most of the funerals were those of old people. I discovered later in life that my paternal aunt's grandchildren, who had died in fairly rapid succession, suffered from malnutrition.

Then while I was doing Form One at Hebron Secondary School, my maternal grandmother in Moiletswane, received a telegraph from Dinokana in Lehurutshe where my uncle was a teacher. The author of the telegraph misinterpreted the message. It was worded, "David Motiang died and will be buried the next day." Moiletswane to Zeerust is quite a long journey especially with lack of regular transport, as was the case in the 1950s.

Grandma's grief was just indescribable. Obviously, she was also puzzled. How could her son die and be buried by strangers the very next day without the next of kin being consulted? Arriving in Dinokana she discovered that it was her grandson who had died. The telegraph had caused the confusion. About three days after the funeral of the baby, and while still at Dinokana, grandma collapsed and died. That was in 1955, and at 16, I was deemed old enough to share in bereavements. In truth I experienced much grief myself, more than I could manage. Because of my vulnerability, the school sent me home with two of my colleagues to attend grandma's funeral. The circumstances of her death caused further grief. It was hard to deal with it. Grandma's funeral resulted in my first visit to a cemetery.

At the time of her death, corpses were kept in morgues. She was kept in Zeerust and then transferred to Brits.

At that time undertakers did not deliver the body on the day preceding the burial. The deceased never lay in their houses on the night before the funeral. Rather, the hearse arrived just when the procession was ready to leave for the cemetery. It could however be that mortuaries were not as advanced then as they are now, in preserving corpses. I cannot tell but what I know is that there was none of the fuss we have today about the corpse being waked at home the night before burial.

Both my grandmothers followed each other to their graves in the same year. The family did not inform me when my paternal grandmother died. Perhaps they felt I was too young to understand.

At Hebron residential students had already formed the custom of accompanying each other to family funerals. On our way from one funeral we stopped momentarily to relieve ourselves. Women who were on their way home from my grandmother's funeral saw us and casually remarked on her passing. What a blow! Grandma and I had been very close. How could anyone not tell me? Our teacher then diverted our route to my home in Polonia where my companions left me. I wept so much, partly because of the loss of grandma, and partly because I had not been informed of her death. The family instantly realised their mistake and instructed my aunt to take me to pay my respects at the grave. In a way I felt better. The following day my father accompanied me back to school.

When my father met his accidental death, I was a boarding mistress at Hebron. My mother was working in Johannesburg as well as was our eldest sister, Suzan. That was in 1965. My brother Behrens was still in a state of frustration after they were incarcerated for the burning of their school. Midah was training as a nurse, which she later abandoned for teacher training. Only my two younger brothers, Lazarus and Abram, were at home. The local teacher phoned Hebron and delivered the sad news. In no time, I was home with my mother who had just arrived. The house was in a mess. My friend from Hebron assisted me in cleaning and putting things in order before mourners arrived to pay their respects. Suzan arrived the same night, much to my relief. The next day both of us visited Avbob's in Brits to identify the corpse, select a coffin and give instructions for its delivery. Still at this stage corpses were delivered on the funeral days. I still remember going to the Lutheran Church during the funeral of my father. The church elder who conducted the service was Dederick Montoedi. He spoke well of my father.

My mother was not fussy about tradition. She wanted to hear from us whether for the funeral, we wished to shave our heads, or not. The decision was ours, and we chose not to remove our hair. The same thing happened after my mother's funeral in 1994. She was no longer there to ask us! Some relatives complained and fretted that we were flouting an important custom, but that was their problem. The values mom had instilled in us made us determined to stand on principle.

Some expressed shock when they saw my hair still intact after burying my mother. What intrigued me was that my two sisters-in-law had shaved their heads. This was their choice and we were not going to take offence.

By the time of my mother's funeral in 1994 traditional mourning customs had completely changed. The family decided to fall in line with modern custom by providing a variety of food: rice, salads, sorghum porridge, juice and cakes for those who had attended the funeral. This was because of the scale of her extended family and being the rakgadi, the first-born. She was much respected by her siblings and their children. At the time of her death she was the only rakgadi, the last to die. These children provided even more in cash and kind than we did. It was a great consolation. They lightened our bereavement.

In my mother's family they do not wait for the next day to wash the clothes of the deceased. My aunts and sisters-in-law started immediately when we arrived home from the cemetery. They did not even put aside her clothes that were to be shared at another special occasion, as was the custom in other families. The next day when everything had been washed and ironed, her clothes were shared among her family members, starting with those closest to her. We were also asked to choose what we needed. I was not interested in anything but was compelled to pick something. I therefore chose one of her best two-piece dresses I had once bought her, and a shawl. She was slender; I can only fit it on when I've lost weight! My grand-daughter values the shawl very much. At first we shared it but as time went on she became more possessive, and refused to let me use it at all. She calls it hers and locks it in her wardrobe when she is away at school. Many other things that belonged to mom were left with my sister. We felt it would be unnecessary for us to remove them.

*Masego granddaughter.*

*My elder sister Midah.*

# The Washing Of Spades

◆

Traditional beer was commonly brewed for funerals, weddings, and other celebrations and feasts. Such celebrations would be the birth of a child, a baptism, confirmation, and when the bogwera returned from circumcision school. People imagined that the ancestors, badimo participated in festivals marked by traditional beer and the slaughter of animals.

Grandma made traditional beer from time to time for grandpa and his peers. Sometimes she provided it as an incentive to the men who had urgent tasks to complete, and complete in good time. One such occasion was harvest time. When the corn was to be stumped to remove the fluff, and to be stored, she also invited men to do it. She would slaughter a sheep or goat and prepare a meal for them. She deemed traditional beer to be an essential ingredient of such a party.

Funerals also provided the perfect excuse for indulging in beer. But the party was thrown a full week after the burial. Such a celebration was poetically called maswe a digarangwe, because it washed the spades that were used to dig the grave of the deceased. Was this not a case of after tears after a week? Nowadays this beer is enjoyed after the meal that follows the funeral, because in our industrialized economy people just cannot wait around for a week, and some have come from afar making a return trip unthinkable.

There was always a supply of corn that was stored for special occasions. When my grandma made traditional beer, she put corn in water. When this corn was wet enough she would remove the excess water and leave it there to grow. Then it was taken out and spread in the sun to dry. The dry corn was now ready to be ground into a meal. For grinding we used a big flat stone, which was a bit rough on the inside, and another smaller stone equally rough.

The corn would be put on the bigger stone and while kneeling we used the smaller stone to grind it. The ground meal would fall onto the clean bag spread around the bigger stone. This meal is called momela. It was then poured into clay pots and put away to ferment. When sour enough, it was ready to be cooked into a soft porridge. This soft porridge was just delicious. You added sugar according to your taste.

Sometimes as the serobo cooks, it foams. This foam can be used to produce a type of porridge called lekwele. You merely place it in another pot and add maize or sorghum meal to harden it a bit. When well cooked it is ready to be eaten. It is very tasty and offers a welcome change to the variety we eat daily.

The brew in the big pots called serobo is poured into big dishes to cool. When it is cool enough, it is thoroughly mixed with cold water and poured into clay pots again. It is covered carefully to maintain the right temperature and after two or three days it is ready to be sifted and strained. As they strain it, the chaff is left aside to feed pigs. The beer is now ready to be drunk.

After sometime the beer foams on top. Grandma would carefully collect the foam and use it to make bread, fat cakes and dumplings.

Beer was regarded as the sole preserve of mature men, and old men of grandpa's age; it partially defined a man's social status. However, some old women also indulged. During my years at Moiletswane, i.e. up to the early 1950s, the elderly women who drank beer were known in the community, simply because they were the exceptions. Even grandma did not fall in the category.

I never saw young men, much less students, drinking beer. The western type of liquor was still rare, and forbidden by law. Black people still did not have the licence to trade liquor as is the case today.

It was later towards the late fifties when a small village called Tshwara started selling liquor. I still do not understand how it all started. But Tshwara was usually known to be a rough area within Makau in those days. When my father and other men went to Makau to attend the kgotla, they had to pass via Tshwara.

It was commonly known that at the kgotla which my dad attended, the right to speak depended on your social status. My father complained that the kgosi's family therefore monopolised the debate. If an ordinary citizen ventured an opinion even on an urgent issue, he'd be soon silenced when the chair made sarcastic reference to liquor. Members, who had come via Tshwara with its notorious liquor sales, were advised not to waste the kgotla's time. My father disliked this kind of bluff which deprived him and his peers of their democratic right to express his opinions.

Tshwara became infamous because of liquor. Little did we know then, that other areas would follow suit. With advancing industrialization, more and more jobs became available in the Vaal Triangle and young people abandoned their rural homes and subsistence farms in tens of thousands. Urbanisation required a totally different lifestyle in which ready cash was essential to survive. You needed madi to pay the rent for your four-roomed matchbox house in Soweto or Mamelodi and to buy smart clothes and groceries and, come to think of it, cigarettes! The latest item in an expanding budget was school fees. Money, money... no wonder some resorted to new and shadier lines of business such as the liquor trade.

Men would soon learn to wash their spades in the newly emerging shebeens, even if graves were now being dug and closed, on contract, by bulldozers. It wasn't grandma's traditional brew either, but stuff that was mass produced and aggressively advertised by South African Breweries. Anyway, would the young generation ever know the difference? Who really cared?

*Solomon, Maggie and Dr Molapo award ceremony.*

# The Badimo Ancestors

◆

During my upbringing at Polonia and Moiletswane, ancestral feasts were not celebrated. However, some of our extended family members practised them regularly. When such occasions were held, all family and extended family were expected to attend. Failure to attend would anger the ancestors. Instead of bringing luck it would be the opposite. The whole ritual would then be deemed a futile exercise.

My mother's belief system did not include ancestral celebrations. Whenever she was invited to such occasions, she refused to attend. Already all family and relatives knew and respected her belief, and because of her, we too avoided such occasions.

It is often said that the education that is best internalised by any child comes from its home. For my mother prayer to God was more important than ancestral beliefs. She often said to us,

> Take care of your parents while they are still alive. If possible give them the best. Support them when they are feeble and cannot manage on their own. See that they are clean and dressed neatly. When they are dead, do not slaughter animals to try to appease them. If you really did what you were supposed to do, it would not be necessary to make feasts to honour them. They would have died happily.

I was once faced with the problem of attending an ancestral feast. When I refused the invitation, I was asked to release my kids to represent the family. They were still young, but I allowed them go. When they returned from the feast, they complained that they were served goat meat with blood clots. They just sampled the porridge. Having never been exposed to such an occasion, they could not sleep. They had stomach cramps and vomited. I felt very guilty. If I could not go, why did I ever allow my kids to go? But I had complied out of respect for other people's beliefs. That was the last time they attended an occasion of that nature.

There are other people who throw parties of all types when in reality the intention is to the ancestors. Of course, if you are invited to a birthday or thanksgiving party you accept, and honour such an invitation.

But the real ancestral feast is held only when the family experiences a lot of problems. The problems are believed to be caused by the ancestor's dissatisfaction and annoyance. People also allege they dream of their forefathers speaking to them and complaining of hunger. Or the ancestors indicate their thirst for blood; so an animal must be sacrificed. Sometimes ancestors intimate that they need a shade over their graves. This is the signal that a deceased near relative wants you to erect a tombstone for him or her. Such nonsense! How can spirits of the dead eat, drink, and feel cold or hot?

The animal to be slaughtered is carefully selected. It cannot be any thing other than the best. Beer is brewed and sorghum meal must be available to make porridge. The whole clan is updated about the intended feast and its purpose. "We want our ancestors to rest. They are angry. We have to appease them." The eldest of the clan must be there when the animal is slaughtered, accompanied by a traditional healer. His basic duty is to address the dead on behalf of the living. He talks to the animal - pleading, appeasing, placating as if addressing the badimo - and then it is slaughtered. The blood is spilt on the ground. This is a good omen, for ancestors will now drink, and quench their thirst. But are we not forgetting the hungry dogs and the crows?

Very early the next day the food is prepared. It has to be ready and eaten before sunrise. Then a sizeable share of the meat, beer, and porridge is taken to the gravesides of the elders who have died. They too have to partake in the feast.

When everybody has eaten, the bones are collected. The bones are not eaten or given to dogs. They must be burnt. A sign that ancestors will enjoy them is the smoke curling upwards. No food must leave the home. Our people are used to eating and carrying some home. But with ancestral feasts no food leaves the yard. People may eat as much as they wish but leave whatever remains.

Depending on instructions from ancestors through dreams or the traditional healer's wisdom, such feasts differ in size and procedure. The family may be asked to bathe together in the same water using herbs to cleanse them of bad luck. They may be asked to spill the beer on the ground instead of taking it to the graves. The family may choose the ox, a goat, sheep, or chicken to be sacrificed. They are often given the colour of the animal to be sacrificed.

The ancestors may still remain angry and unappeased in spite of all the trouble taken. In this case a family has to make an introspection of what might have gone wrong. Perhaps the wrong elder was chosen to represent the family. The family might have omitted certain members from their invitation list or else something that was supposed to be done as communicated was not followed to the letter.

It is believed that in their anger ancestors could cause a lot of conflict within a family such as disunity, violence, divorces, accidents, deaths, bareness, and problems at work, or even failure to find a job. For people whose ancestral beliefs are very strong it is often difficult to draw the line between God and the ancestors.

Obviously black people in pre-Christian Africa societies did not worship God in the same manner as we do today. But they believed that there was a certain power above their ancestors, the Supreme Power. They believed it was only through the ancestors that they could communicate with this power. They reasoned that the Supreme Being was "up there in the heavens". In their language godimo literally means up there; hence Modimo, meaning God. Thus we see our Batswana ancestors were Theists, believing in one God.

Is it not now clear to us that God was at work among us Africans before ever a missionary set foot in Africa!

As with other Christians, we in the Catholic Church have begun this process of 'enculturation' in our attempt to integrate African beliefs with the Christian message. We are trying to reconcile the two main cultures.

From the earliest centuries the Christian community has remained in communion with the generations gone before them in death, "marked with the sign of Faith". The spiritual bond with the souls of the departed is strengthened in another way too. The Christian community has always honoured the memory of persons who were outstanding for their holiness of life. These are men and women from all ranks of life who lived Christ-like lives. They are presented as models to be imitated. For about the last 1 000 years, the church has been formally declaring such holy persons to be saints, in a ceremony called canonisation. A modern example is Mother Teresa, who will likely be canonised very soon.

The Christian belief is that the church, the body of Christ, comprises three parts: we believers on pilgrimage through this world; our saved ancestors already in heaven; and thirdly, those ancestors undergoing purification for entry into heaven. All three groups are in spiritual communion, the Communion of Saints.

Because the saints are in the presence of God, we beg them to pray to God on our behalf. We pray for our loved ones that they may be soon purified enough to enter heaven. We pray to the saints, but we pray for the souls who are on their way. This way we maintain communion with past generations, and indeed with all the people of God.

Why therefore should we black Christians be so secretive about worshipping our ancestors? Rather we might think of inviting a suitable priest to participate in these rites. Life for our loved ones is only changed; it is not taken away. Yes, our prayers can reach them. We are in closest communion with them at Mass when the biblical Lamb of God offers himself for the sins of all humankind.

We believe that different events in our families are blessed if we invoke our ancestors. A wedding where lobola is paid is said to be a contract between the two families and the ancestors. In this way the union is blessed. The initial lobola was paid by the groom's family in the form of cattle. The cattle themselves, part of God's creation, were understood by our ancestors to strengthen the bonds of marriage.

People were given names known to their ancestors. Whenever they address their ancestors, they would identify themselves, "I'm so and so…", followed by the ancestral name. Thus, I was taught to believe that a name like Maggie would not be recognised by my ancestors. But if I identify myself as Mampee or Machinto my ancestors would readily listen because they'd recognise who addressed them.

Families also have their praise songs, which have been passed on to them by word of mouth from generation to generation. Whenever these family praise songs are rendered, ancestors' names are included. Hence they also become part of the praise.

My sister Midah's ancestral name is Mamadi. Our praise song mentions the name "Mamadi". Grandma usually called her "Mantsebe" and this "Mantsebe" is also mentioned in the praise song of our family. This goes to say that "Mamadi a Ntsebe must have been one of the influential women in our family". This praise song for an industrious family goes on like this:

*Ke bana ba Mamadi a Ntsebe*
*Ke bana ba Mmamarotse matala a kwa Pholotse*
*Ba ba reng marotse matala a kwa Motlhosane*
*Ke bana ba segagaripa sa mogoma*

*Ke batlola mafura a motlouwane*
*Ba ba se keng ba a tlola ba lebagane*
*Ke bana ba Mmamoletsane-mosesanyane*
*Tlhoka mofolledi.*
*Re ba rakgamo ya tsala motsileng*
*Motlhana o sale o jewa ke magokobu*
*O jewa ke dibatana tsa naga*

*They are the children of Mamadi-the-child-of-Ntsebe.*
*They are the mothers of green pumpkins found at Pholose,*
*Who say green pumpkins can be found also at Motlhosane.*
*They are the children of a sharp plough.*

*They are those that apply the fat of the motlouwane tree.*
*Who do not apply it facing one another.*
*They are the children of the Mother-of-Moletsane-the-slim-one.*
*So thin, like a thin needle difficult to thread.*
*We are those of a cow who gives birth in the wilderness.*
*The placenta left to be eaten by vultures and wild animals.*

Praise songs are sung at weddings to honour the one getting married. They are also chanted at funerals to praise the deceased and thus connect him/her with the ancestors. Praise songs may be sung for any important family function. The right to render the song rests with the paternal aunt or maternal uncle.

Because our paternal aunts are all deceased my sister and I sing these songs on behalf of the family. We naturally exercise this duty towards our brothers' children.

A praise song is sacred, and commands respect. People are attentive when it is sung. It reveals who this person really is, and where he/she originates. Because many people are related without knowing it, it is at times like this that you suddenly discover you have a new relative.

Women ululate when the praise song is sung. The mood can turn melancholy and some are reduced to tears. The one who is being honoured sometimes cries too. The song describes you to yourself telling you who you are. I find it important for every person to know who he or she is and where they come from. After all you might live in a community, but you could have been born elsewhere. Your praise song therefore might introduce you to a new land.

Praise songs were also composed in honour of warriors who won a battle. Dikgosi are showered with praise poems all the time; in the kgotla there was always a royal praise singer. His duty was to praise and flatter the kgosi at the opening of the kgotla, when he made his speech, or when overwhelmed with something good he had achieved.

Like the praise singer, the kgosi had one or two traditional healers. Their duty was to see that everything was in order when the kgosi vacated his house; that he was safe at kgotla or anywhere he went. They had to throw the bones to test the water and so ensure their kgosi was safe. Should the king for some reason, meet a mishap, the community would take the traditional healers to task. They could even be punished with death if they betrayed the tribe's trust.

Ancestors have been part of every aspect of the lives of black people. A baby that was born after several of his/her siblings had died was referred to as ngwana wa badimo, the child of the ancestors. When they grew up in our communities such children were handled with great care. They were regarded as being highly vulnerable. They easily fell sick. As a precaution a large safety pin was fastened to the child's hair. You'd immediately notice that you could not even touch the child. To touch him/her you had to make a donation in either cash or kind. The child would also be given an unusual, or even derogatory name. It was believed in that way he/she would survive. The name Matlakala means dirt.

A German missionary could bear this out. His infants did not survive. The community advised him that when his wife gave birth again, he should allow them to select a name for the new-born. When in due course his wife gave birth they gave the child a Tswana name. They called her Segwagwa, frog. The child survived to adulthood.

People who suddenly amass wealth are said to be given it by their ancestors. In other words, their ancestors are pleased with them. But in that case they owe their ancestors a thank-you feast. A beast must be slaughtered so that the ancestors may bless them more. Should the lucky family fail to thank them, the belief is that all their riches could be taken away from them.

There are stories of people being called by ancestors when they die. Some people who were near death but survived are said to have been sent back by ancestors. Sometimes, according to the storytellers, the ancestors appeal to the dying one not to abandon their children as orphans.

My grandma once told me a story of two brothers. One brother, Rapula, was blessed with a number of children, many of whom were boys. The other brother Mosimane, had only one child a son. One day this one son fell seriously ill. For sometime the parents tried everything they could to save the boy's life. Early one morning the boy said to his mother that his grandmother was calling him. The grandmother had died many years before. But his mother was furious with the granny calling their only son.

She scolded him: "But how could she do that? Why is she so cruel to us? She could have gone to Rapula's family where there are so many children and taken one of them."

Unfortunately that boy died. The couple was left childless while Rapula still remained with his many children. The ancestors had made their choice, according to grandma.

My mother fell seriously ill one day and was admitted to hospital. Really there was no hope. But she came out of that illness. She related a story to us. In her dream she saw my paternal grandmother and my father. Both of them talked to her. They instructed her to go back to the children. The next day she felt so well that she was discharged from hospital.

I have never had the luck of speaking to, or been spoken to, by my ancestors, except one night while in prison. I was actually half asleep, half awake. My father stood there supporting himself against the burglar door of my cell. He asked me, "How are they going to try you in court when the others are absent?" I later related this to my colleague, Fanny, who with me, was charged with sedition. Well, it was just a dream we both agreed. After we were released on bail, and before we went to court the first time, Fanny disappeared - nowhere to be found. We later learnt that she had fled the country and gone to Tanzania. Her absence made my case much lighter. The defence advocate argued that I could not be tried in the absence of my accomplice. I was therefore acquitted. The state's case was flawed in other serious ways too, and it just fell apart.

*Harold in matric at Tsogo High School receiving a science award to London.*

# Death And Burial Rites Today

---

$\blacklozenge$

---

Bereavements nowadays have been turned into social gatherings. People meet their long lost friends and relatives. They are aware that most of them will meet again only when one of them dies.

Worst of all, funerals have become competitive. People want their funerals to be better organised than others. The food that is prepared is really so unnecessary for the occasion. Since most funerals are conducted in the morning, women have to start cooking long before dawn so as to have a funeral meal ready for the returning mourners. But when you look at the heavily laden tables, it is not what we normally eat for breakfast. It is a lunch menu, served at 9 o'clock in the morning! There is a lot of wastage as people do not eat so much at that time of the day. Among the latest additions, is the "after tears". Crates of liquor are served after the meal. But grief is a process. It cannot heal just after the burial of a loved one. The "after tears" fashion is therefore absurd, to say the least.

The unveiling of tombstones and the parties accompanying the occasion are also a relatively new custom for us blacks. When I was growing up the unveiling of tombstones was never celebrated. We saw tombstones erected only in the cemeteries of whites, but they never threw parties to unveil them. In my view the concept of tombstones is not bad in itself. After all, a tombstone is a useful grave marker. It serves as a memorial symbol, a reminder to future generations that here lies a father, mother, and grandfather, grandmother who was born on such a day, and died on such a day. As for parties, why not leave them to those who can afford them?

Tombstone like funerals themselves are now big business and have become established status symbols. They have also given rise to a new breed of criminal, whether a thief or a plain vandal. At dead of night these thugs remove or destroy expensive tombstones, thus increasing the misery of those who erected them. Perhaps that is a reminder to think again before wasting money on expensive graves. Suppose our loved ones were to return to earth with just one request, which would they ask for: a showy new tombstone or a donation to a charitable cause in their name?

When cemeteries are properly attended to they reflect well both on the living, and on the dead. Neatly trimmed graveyards adorned with flowers and shrubs add to the beauty of the immediate environment. They inspire us to visit the gravesides of loved ones and perhaps to pray that they rest in peace. I have nothing against tombstones that are modest, and accommodate themselves to the ordinary people. Is the cemetery ever a place to show off one's social status?

I admire the Czechs and Poles for the way they maintain their cemeteries. At first I was not even sure that I was passing a cemetery. They are in effect, beautiful gardens with tombstones. Flowers are planted between and among the tombstone. Could not we too turn our graveyards into flower gardens and even renovate old, abandoned sites?

The forced removals in South Africa have turned old graveyards into deserted sites. Sometimes the new areas are far from the families who have to go back to erect tombstones. In 1986, we travelled in two buses from Ramogodi to the old Moiletswane to unveil my grandparents' tombstones. The site was deserted and desolate. We moved among bushes and tall, wild grass to reach the graves. There were no roads and the buses had to stop a distance from the cemetery.

Again in 1993, we travelled from Ramogodi to unveil the tombstone of my father at the old Polonia where he was buried before the forced removals. The experience was the same.

There is rivalry of another kind involved with funerals. It concerns our tit-for-tat attitude regarding actual attendance. If you don't attend my family funeral, I'll not attend yours! Similarly if you fail to turn up for duty at a funeral occasion the aggrieved family will likely take a very poor view of your absence and accuse you of negligence. This attitude falls short of the ubuntu or botho which we proclaim all the time.

When you look at the number of funerals today, it isn't possible for anyone to make an appearance at all of them. You may attend many funerals in your lifetime but that does not guarantee that the same people will be at yours. Many will have passed on, but new faces will appear to take their places. Going to a funeral, paying our respects to the bereaved, offering assistance are acts of charity. You perform these acts in a spirit of condolence and charity and as a humanitarian gesture. Can bereavements ever be occasions for small-minded tokens of revenge?

When two people of unequal status die, the tendency is for the majority to flock to the one of higher rank. I cannot forget the challenge I was faced with one day when two acquaintances of mine died. One was my neighbour's wife; the other was a person of high social standing. Their funerals also occurred on the same day. I opted to stay mainly with my grieving neighbours, thus ignoring the expectations of the wealthier family. Some of the latter who seemed enslaved by the demands of social status did not take kindly to my absence.

I sometimes ask myself what impact religious faith is exerting on our society. South Africa is a multi-faith country. Whatever faith we profess, it should help liberate us from the vanities that ensnare us, vanities that rear their ugly heads in the form of ostentatious tombstones, and funeral fashions and rivalries in general. It is the ordinary citizens struggling to make ends meet, who are most threatened by these latter day trends. They feel compelled to conform, and at all costs to keep up appearances.

In pre-Christian times our ancestors were good and caring people. They received foreigners; they helped the sick and fed the poor. They offered all the necessary help irrespective of who needed it.

The dress code at funerals is also alarming. My belief is that a funeral differs from all other family and social occasions. The dress codes of mourners are best when they reflect the sombre mood of the occasion. Are cemeteries ever the places for mini-skirts, high heels, flashy cosmetics, and loud perfumes? And when it comes to the sensitive issue of colour, is black, in this context, not truly beautiful?

A friend of mine once told me that she could not attend a funeral of a colleague because she did not have a hat to wear. I wear a doek at funerals.

The programmes for some funerals are unnecessarily long. I agree that people want to celebrate the life of the deceased, to remind the community about the good works and achievements of the deceased, and to hail his/her success in life. But my question is this, why wait till people die? Should we not initiate a ceremony where we gather and praise our living heroes and heroines instead of letting them die first?

Our agendas set forth the list of speakers and inevitably there is much repetition. I suggest that the MC tactfully reminds successive speakers to avoid repeating each other. Should we continue speaking just because we are scheduled to, or should we speak because there is something new to be added? Sometimes when a so-called important person suddenly appears among the mourners, he/she even though not on the prepared list, is handed the microphone. How appropriate is such a 'pecking order' at ceremonies which remind us of our one most basic common, human limitation: our mortality? Shakespeare puts it wisely,

Sceptre and crown shall tumble down

And in the dust be equal made.

Perhaps the late-coming VIP should volunteer to speak last, because late-coming itself can send a very mixed cultural signal.

Speakers at gravesides tend to monopolise the ceremony, turning into a secular event. The church's role which is to ensure the religious character of the funeral, is today being afforded less and less space, and in most cases is ignored. Some mourners prefer to stand outside and mix socially, mobiles fully active, long before the priest has concluded his rites. Their chatter competes with the prayers. Yet there is a time for everything.

*Chris Puff (my niece's husband) and my mother,*
*Martha Maadimo*

# Part Four
# **Educator**

# Joys And Sorrows,
# Joys And Sorrows

◆

During 1956, I was doing Form Three, or J.C. Today we refer to this level as Standard Eight or even Grade Ten. My classmates had gone through two levels, namely Form One and Two, while I had come straight from Form One. Whenever my peers talked to me I was left with a sense of discouragement. This motivated me, however, rather than disheartened me. I worked very hard from the beginning and by mid-year examinations, it was already clear to everybody in class that I was an excellent student. Once more I topped them all. I appreciated the trust that my teachers placed upon me and I was not one to disappoint them.

At the end of the year in the final examinations, I was the only one who registered for English A. Again my classmates tried to frighten me out of this decision but I would not budge. When the results were finally announced, I had passed English A with a good symbol, and distinctions in both Arithmetic and History. But where was I to go from here? That had been a problem from day one when I arrived at Hebron. I wanted to go somewhere for Matric but my mother was struggling to make ends meet. She would ask her employer to pay her salary two months in advance, so that she could pay for our fees. That meant she would be working for two months without payment. She could hardly buy anything decent for herself.

Fortunately for her, she was in the women's prayer group of the Lutheran Church. This helped her. Even if she did not have smart clothes to wear she at least had a prayer uniform, which she wore on Thursdays and Sundays when she attended church services. On the other weekdays she wore the uniform provided by her employer. At the beginning of 1957 the Mmanotshe Moduane Secondary School, which had been running a three-year course leading to the Teachers' Certificate, requested me to join the final year of that course. This was because of my academic record. Given my financial plight, I immediately consented to this request. It was a boring exercise, not challenging enough for me but I persevered in spite of all the pitfalls. At the end of the year I graduated with both the J.C. and the Teachers' Certificate.

Those were the days of school boards. A school board secretary would decide who to employ and who to refuse. Although I applied for a teaching post quite early, I got no response. My school performance was also very good. I approached the school board secretary thinking that he would recall receiving my application letters. On talking to him I was extremely disappointed when he listed the applicants. He did not even attempt to disguise that they were getting posts because of their family backgrounds. He did not reveal their names but referred to them as so-and-so's daughter.

Knowing the status of my parents, I realized that unless I chose some remote place I would not get employed at all. I also tried the township in Brits where I received a warm welcome. But at the end I received no positive response even though they were short of teachers. Finally, I accepted a position at Peela, some 85km west of Rustenburg. I had to board a train for Rustenburg at our local station, Dewildt. From Rustenburg I boarded a bus to take me to Peela. It was raining very hard that day. The bus had a leaking roof, leaving me soaked to the skin in that long trip. Another unpleasant thing was that the bus was full beyond its capacity. I did not know where I was going; I had to rely on the passengers in the bus. I was still only 18 years of age, and very vulnerable. At Peela I was immediately assisted with my baggage, and shown to the accommodation that had been arranged for me by the school.

I stayed with an elderly couple, but the old lady was still working in Johannesburg as a domestic servant. After telling her where my mother worked, she visited her and they soon became friends.

At Peela, I started teaching the Sub As, today Grade One. It was a pleasure teaching this class indeed. I could sing, jump and dance with them. My principal was very pleased with me. When he had visitors, he brought them to my class. Visitors were especially brought in to view my classroom as the walls were covered from corner to corner with teaching and learning aids. He appreciated this very much and even during weekends when he took rounds with his visitors, he was sure to bring them to my classroom.

But I was later changed to a Standard Two class and towards the end of the year to Standard Four.

I was also involved with the Sunbeams and Wayfarers clubs, basketball training, an intermediate choir and a quartet. It was a pity because I had to leave at the end of the year.

It is amazing how we survived during those days with the meagre salaries we received. When I started teaching I was paid ten guineas, which is £10/10 per month or about R120 today. Yet I was able to clothe myself well, buy food and even send a few shillings home every month. I also had the luxury of owning a wristwatch!

I have to admit though, that life was very simple then. In the evenings I cooked porridge, and fried eggs mixed with onions and sometimes tomatoes as well. That would be my supper. Eggs were very cheap in a rural community. Sometimes I bought tinned fish or corn beef to go with the pap. There was no butchery in the village at the time. Unless we bought meat of home-slaughtered animals, we would wait for transport to Madikoe, or undertake a month-end trip to Rustenburg.

There was a family store that made bread, which was delicious. They made small loaves that cost six pence each. That was enough to last me for at least two days. We did not bring any food to school, but instead formed a tea club. We either bought bread from this family store or got fat-cakes supplied to us regularly by a kind lady. We paid her monthly from our tea club contributions.

Weddings in the village usually took place on weekdays, and many marriages were not blessed in church. They were mostly traditional where the paying of lobola in itself was enough to constitute a legal marriage. During such wedding days our principal would just send word for the staff to be supplied with lunch. The meals were simple - sour sorghum porridge, with beef. The women felt honoured to bring the meals to their local teachers.

As a teacher I would receive a lot of friends in the house, but the old man was totally against this. One day as I was doing routine cleaning I broke a vase. On reporting this, he said we should wait for its owner to return from Johannesburg. The day after she arrived I reported this to her. I had never seen such fury! She stressed how hard she had worked to buy the ornament. I apologised and enquired how much compensation she wanted. She mentioned such a huge amount that I realized right there that the family did not really want me. I was not one of them.

When I prepared my own food, my culture forbade me to eat without sharing with the old man, though this fell outside the terms of our agreement.

One day he had slaughtered a sheep and was selling the mutton. He asked me to buy for myself before it got finished. I did so. I cooked this meat with pap. Again conscience would not allow me to eat my food alone. I dished out for him although he had made me buy the meat. He welcomed the food without any remarks.

I was very young when I started teaching - I was still in my teens. I found boys and girls my own age in Standard Six. This did not bother me much. School children were still very obedient. They treated me with respect. But my colleagues always reminded me of my peer group in the school. At leisure times they would make insinuating remarks about this. After the school concerts on Saturday nights, a group of Standard Six boys would be assigned to see me safely back to my apartment. A group of them would accompany me and make sure my room was safely locked before leaving.

When still a student, I looked very smart and dignified in my gym dress and my long-sleeved, white shirt; my hair was usually plaited. I loved this sports attire and wore it to school. That was something these scholars had not experienced before. They just glared at me, but I was proud because I knew that I looked beautiful in that outfit. Jokingly, my principal called the staff after assembly and suggested that I be given a desk in one of the Standard Six classes. Generally they all felt that I had done something they had never thought of. They recognized it as my way of encouraging neatness and cleanliness among the pupils. Thinking of it now, I wonder what might happen to me. Today some teachers and pupils have no respect for one another. There are many reports of sexual offences among teachers and learners. Would I be safe today, I often ask myself.

I had never been warned by the elderly couple that after sunset I was not allowed to bring water to the house. Sometimes schoolwork delayed me and I'd arrive late at the house. I had to draw water from the village pump to use for cooking, drinking and washing. On one occasion when I arrived with a pail of water I was forbidden to enter the yard, as it was after sunset. I was desperate. I had to do without food that night. Early the next day I had to fetch water to wash myself before going to school. When the school closed for the quarter, my colleagues found me a new accommodation at another part of the village.

As winter approached it was time boys and girls who were peer groups of the kgosi's son, to attend circumcision school. The chief himself announced at school that some of our scholars would be going through this cultural ritual. The chief's son was a pupil in Standard Four.

We were at assembly one morning when the group to be circumcised passed the school wrapped in blankets and singing dikoma, adult male songs. It was a moment filled with anxiety and apprehension for my scholars. It was as if they were dead in their desks. In my ignorance of what awaited the bogwera, I could not figure out anything of what was happening. Such a culture shock for the girl from Polonia! Not every family has the good luck of seeing their sons back in good health, or even alive. The misfortunes connected to this cultural practice, however, may not be compared to the gains: adulthood.

When the bogwera returned from the mountains there was rejoicing, feasting, dancing and ululating. But some families were left in mourning.

The kgosi once more visited the school to announce that now that his son had been through circumcision, he has to be respected as a man. I came to their class as usual to order the boys to leave the classroom, as they had to do gardening, and the girls had to attend to their needlework. The kgosi's son was in this particular class and to the amazement of all, the boys remained seated. I called again and received a similar reaction.

Some girls whispered, "They say they are not boys." I had to do or say something to wriggle out of this embarrassing event, and avoid a serious confrontation. So I challenged, "If you are men, are you perhaps my men? You know I've got work to do in this class in your absence." The message struck home; they left the classroom without a word, much to my relief. I had avoided a riot, a riot of passage!

# Tlhabane On Trial

◆

$B$ethel Training College is situated near a dorpie called Coligny. From Bodenstein Station you needed private transport to get to the college.

Many parents during those days thought that sending children to remote boarding schools provided a real advantage. But Bethel, like all boarding schools, expelled students for such irregularities as teenage pregnancies and truancy.

There was a primary school in the small village next to the college, where student teachers did their practical teaching. After my marriage I lived at the teachers' residence in Bethel and found employment at the Teaching Practice School.

The Lutheran Church in the village would be filled to capacity during the normal running of the college. During school holidays it was attended by two to five villagers. As we walked back to our residence, we would come upon groups of men, young and old, enjoying their liquor. The women would be busy with their usual chores.

One Sunday on our way from the church service, we visited a family and enquired about the non-commitment to church displayed by some villagers. Their response was that people had used the Bible to grab the land from them and that they no longer had confidence in the church. This did not make much sense to me.

It was a winter morning when bulldozers were flattening houses, and properties were being carted off. The villagers were moved against their will to a remote, infertile area in exchange for the farms they occupied - and had bought. But what had gone wrong? Like most blacks in South Africa, Bethel people had confidence in the missionaries. When this small community bought its land, leaders relied on the local missionary to do the paperwork on their behalf since they were illiterate. What happened during the process, only the missionaries themselves can explain. It is hard, however to figure out what exactly happened. In the end they were told the land belonged to the Lutheran Church Missionaries.

In line with the political changes in South Africa after 1994, this small community, like all other communities in the country, successfully reclaimed their land.

When I was pregnant with my second child Olivia, I took maternity leave. Unfortunately I could not go back to my job. A new clause in the women teachers' contract stipulated that when a married woman went for maternity leave she would be replaced by a single one immediately. Basically what it meant was that I no longer had a post. However, there had been overpayments on my part from the Department of education in Pretoria. The only way I could refund these overpayments was to be re-employed. So I was fortunate enough to go back to my job until my family moved to Potchefstroom where my husband had been offered a principal's post at Tlokwe Secondary School. But soon, local politics at the secondary school became a hindrance. He could cope for only two years. This forced us to move to Hebron College where he was offered a post. Kilnerton College, a Methodist institution, which like all other excellent, church-related centres of learning in the country, had closed and moved to Hebron.

The only job available to me was that of a boarding mistress in the boys' residence. I loved this job from the beginning since it offered me economic security, and the opportunity to further my studies. At the same time I could raise my children comfortably without having to hire someone to look after them. It was a challenging job, having to cater for the needs of boys, some of them men already. I had to see to it that they were properly fed. When they were ill I'd move them to the sick room, and either administer conventional medicine which was always available in the dispensary; or I would refer them to a nursing sister at the local clinic. In time our hostel residents were like one big family for us. I also had to monitor the cleanliness and hygiene of the whole area. Workers doing this job reported to me.

School holidays were not something I looked forward to. The whole place suddenly became a ghost town. In my endeavour to fight this boredom, I would take the children to town for a day, invite visitors, or go visiting friends and family coming back only to sleep. I held this Hebron post from 1965 to 1971 and during this period I studied very hard to improve my life. First I studied for, and passed Matric. Next, I enrolled with the University of South Africa, UNISA. My working schedule was flexible enough to allow me to visit the library of the university, to study, to consult books and lecturers, as well as do assignments on a regular basis.

Indeed when I quit in June 1971, I was left with only two courses to complete my BA. At Tlhabane Training School, where I found a similar position vacant, I stayed for six months. There the social environment was very different from that of Hebron; it was also quite volatile. I immediately realized that this post was not meant for me, and I made preparations to leave at the end of that year. Little did I know that one day I'd come back to this institution not as a boarding mistress but as lecturer, after the institution was upgraded to a college of education in 1983.

The head of Tlhabane College and quite a number of his staff came from Bethel Training College where they had taught after we left for Potchefstroom. When the college closed and was later converted to a high school, most of the staff moved to Rustenburg to start the Tlhabane Training School. They formed a closely-knit group who in my judgment did not easily accommodate anyone from outside. I could not get myself used to the manner in which the student hostels were run. I felt that nobody who did not belong could tolerate the partiality the head of the college displayed. However, some of my black colleagues seemed quite happy. I viewed it as a real divide-and-rule sort of thing. I felt I had become the black sheep of this Tlhabane flock. I soon realized that remaining in a situation like that would harm me and my children's development. My children were becoming restless; I felt very guilty for having exposed them to such negative attitudes.

# Tshukudu High School: Cheers And Tears

◆

When I resigned from Tlhabane Training School I was faced with a challenge at Bafokeng High School. This was 1972 and here was I returning to the classroom after an eight-year absence. The difference here was that now I was qualified for the challenges of high school teaching. Knowing the importance of classroom competence, I worked hard at preparation of my lessons. I taught Form II (Grade Nine today) English and Social Studies. There were four classes with between 80 and 100 in each classroom for both my subjects. The load was heavier than anyone could anticipate. For example, a single written assignment left me with 400 exercise books to mark! I persevered.

Later this load was further increased when I was given English in Form Four and Setswana in Form Five respectively. The most pleasant memories of teaching during these years were the unconditional co-operation of students and the appreciation of parents. At this school we had teachers who worked hard and were punctual, who gave written work and evaluated it, and who did not rely on the cane to make students work or force them into submission. During those days we packed students' assignments in paper bags, for marking. The following day you returned with it complete, and carried a second bag also. The principal of the school was a man of very few words, and never a slave-driver. Hence most of us worked hard - not just to please him - but because we were duty bound and answering our calling.

At the end of 1974, I obtained my BA. There were a number of junior secondary schools, which started up at the beginning of 1975. Before I could celebrate my achievement, I was called upon to head Tshukudu Secondary School in Bleskop. The school started with 80 learners in Form I - Grade Eight - in two classrooms which we were loaned by Photsaneng Primary School. The new buildings were still in the process of completion and were situated between Photsaneng and Thekwana; the idea was to serve both areas.

When I was first introduced to the community, they looked at me not only as a woman, but as a young person. I was only 36, and they anxiously enquired whether I could cope. My response, which seemed not to come from me, but from an inner voice, was unbelievable, "I will cope - but only with your support" I had been praying.

Indeed, it must have come from an inner voice. I do not even want to explain the quality of support I received from these two communities, without which I could hardly have managed.

The Photsaneng Primary School principal offered the use of both his offices for both schools. I was a teacher, a principal, and a clerk  all rolled into one. At the beginning I was offered only one assistant teacher. During the following year the school was granted three extra posts. Things started to normalize when the new buildings were completed and we moved in. The men and women who were elected to serve in the school council were committed; they proved very reliable. They were my pillars of strength. Today there is an outcry that parents are less involved in their children's education, but this is not what I experienced at Tshukudu Secondary School. However that was 30 years ago. This parents' representative body did not wait for the principal to call them. They came at any time just to find out where their assistance was required. I owe my achievements to all the parents of the children I taught there, and particularly to the school council. Both young and old generally addressed me as "Ma'am." This community was really proud of their school. They loved it. Calling a parents' meeting was never a problem. They attended in great numbers.

This school served the villages of Photsaneng, Thekwana, and Mfidikwe, as well as the mines and adjacent farms. However, we also admitted children from as far afield as Mabieskraal, Phokeng and Tlhabane. Tshukudu Secondary School's name and fame spread all over because of its achievements.

During the Soweto uprising in 1976, there was an exodus of students from the townships to rural areas. Tshukudu Secondary School in Rustenburg became a major rendezvous point. We admitted many students who were introduced by relatives and friends. Although there were some parents and teachers who feared the discipline of the school would be affected, it never was.

The riots of 1976 negatively affected many rural schools and colleges, but not Tshukudu. People kept asking me what I did to be so organized in the midst of so much chaos. In addition to the strong parental support structures, I suggest that I was at peace with myself. Harmony, like charity, begins at home, does it not?

What hurt me grievously was that all these achievements did not impress the powers that prevailed in Mafikeng. For some reason, I always remained a thorn in their flesh. Part of the problem was that my school council and I refused permission for the ruling party of Bophuthatswana to hold their meetings on our premises. No political party would enjoy such a privilege. We said it straight: no political meetings would be held in our school. This policy we knew would have far-reaching consequences; and indeed its effects followed me throughout, until finally the government of Bophuthatswana was overthrown - eighteen years later.

The school, young though it was, excelled in everything. We were in the vicinity of the Rustenburg Platinum Mines and even before we had developed sports facilities of our own, our students were training at the mine's facilities. The school produced champion athletes and netball players who are actively engaged in sports to this day.

Our first Standard Eight results were the best in the region. This in turn allowed us to establish the practice of celebrating results in order to better motivate our students and staff. This first one was a big feast. An ox was slaughtered. The community and the whole circuit came to celebrate with us. During the following year, our school's results were not only the best in the circuit; they were quality results. Names of top achievers appeared in the media. They were the best in the country. It was such a rewarding experience! Teachers were elated. Of course they had reason to celebrate. Hard workers, they never left anything to chance. Among this first group of learners my daughter, Magae, excelled; she was one of the best. The following year my last-born, Harold, obtained a distinction with As and a few Bs. His name appeared in the print media of the country. Another girl, Refiloe, also made headlines. I still maintain that only those teachers who allow their own children to attend the schools where they are employed, can rate themselves highly. It is an acid test.

Communities have faith in such teachers. The good results and achievements in sports became a tradition of Tshukudu High School. We introduced Matric at the school but before we could come to terms with this major move, the Government of Bophuthatswana decided to remove me from my post. The community tried to fight this decision but failed.

I enquired whether I'd have the same position where I was transferred. The official answer I was given that it was not in the Department's interest to see whether or not I was placed in that position.

Herman Thebe High School in Matau had a notorious reputation. Principals were changing yearly. When I got there, there was no principal; the principal's office did not have a single file for reference. I started new files as in a newly established school. The teachers were not as dedicated as at Tshukudu but they appreciated my guidance.

Few people will know about the tears I shed when I was forced, without any reason, to leave the school I had founded. My tears were not shed in public though, because I was determined that no matter how powerful the authorities were at that time, they were not going to break me. My family was equally appalled and disappointed. In fact their pain was greater than my own. From that time onwards, my children were wary of living in Bophuthatswana.

At Herman Thebe High School I taught English to Standard Nine and Ten. The students were totally against my introduction of poetry. I promised them they were going to enjoy it. In a short time their attitude changed. Today I still have some of them, men and women, thanking me for having introduced them to poetry.

I had never been a mamoratwa, a blue-eyed baby of the government of Bophuthatswana. Even at the time I was producing top results at Tshukudu, the government was not impressed. To nip me in the bud, they decided to terminate my employment and I was left to find myself a school in the Madikoe region.

Worse was to follow. I had hardly been at Herman Thebe High School for three months when the officials from the department arrived and accused me of having misappropriated an amount of R12 000 since I was principal of Herman Thebe High School.

Having collected all the receipts from the school I handed them over to my clerk to file them. This would serve as evidence to show them how every cent was spent. However, these officials destroyed the receipts. Then they told the clerk not to report their mischief. That way only Mrs Bopalamo, who was the accounting officer would be charged. Nevertheless, the clerk did inform me. Although these officials threatened to charge her with the same misdeed as mine, she went ahead and reported to me what had happened. Still they had the audacity to interrogate the clerk as to why she informed me.

There was no irregularity at Tshukudu and the school was running smoothly. It would seem these officials were just trying their luck to discredit me.

I was summoned to the head office. The intention was to force me to sign an undertaking to refund the missing money. I stared at the group of men who filled that office and who were coercing me to sign. I refused. I did however; agree to return the following week. But, return I did not. Instead, I wrote them a letter detailing all the irregularities of their investigation. That was the last time I heard of them - to this day.

After many years of absence at music competitions, Herman Thebe High School choirs made their re-appearance. Their comeback was a real break-through. The school had boarding facilities, which were controlled by the community. I decided to leave my accommodation at the student's residence and find myself a place elsewhere.

I did not want to be mixed up in local politics. The first accommodation I was offered was a house next to the clinic, which belonged to the Department of Health.

One Sunday night I arrived back to find the house flooded. There was no one to help me; it was too late. I finally went to sleep in the small hours. As if that incident wasn't enough, I was ordered to vacate the house immediately as it belonged to the Department of Health.

Once more I was faced with a crisis. My new accommodation consisted of a single room far away from the school; this I used for cooking and sleeping. The weather was hot and dry although it was supposed to be the rainy season. Travelling to school was real torture.

My clerk was Mrs. Sekano, an elderly lady, seasoned and hardworking. She really gave me all the support I needed. When I arrived at Herman Thebe High School she had recently lost her husband and was still in mourning. She gave me many insights into the traditions and customs of the area, and she also related some unpleasant things she had to endure after the death of her spouse.

According to local tradition of the Bakwena, a woman in mourning had to stay indoors for a period of a year. She informed me that when she was bored, she would request her children to bring her their laundry so that she could wash it in the bedroom. She would then ask them to hang it outside. She was not supposed to be seen even in her own yard.

As her husband had worked and stayed in Johannesburg, now Gauteng, they owned another house in Soweto. After her husband's burial, it was permissible enough for her to go to Soweto to pack some of his belongings, bring them home, and then make arrangements regarding the house.

Tradition did not allow her to be seen in the village, much less to go beyond it. The only sensible thing to do was to approach the kgotla through the kgosi to lift these restrictions. After protracted debates at the kgotla she was finally allowed to leave the village and also move about. However, the majority of villagers were totally against this decision.

When the poor woman came back to the village, there was an outcry. Villagers complained that there would be no rain because a mourning woman was allowed to flout their traditions and cross their cultural boundaries. It was a coincidence that there was a drought that year. The tribe lived on subsistence farming but that year crops just withered in the fields, for lack of rain. There was no harvest. Her story was interesting and touching. Yet the drought in the village was blamed on her.

She also got permission from the kgotla to work in order to maintain her children who were still in school. Some students who came from conservative families avoided her; others had no problem. Of course at school I referred students to the clerk for certain things affecting them, leaving them no choice. After all, she was employed by the school as a clerk and that was that.

From the time I arrived at the school, I was determined that I would spend only a year there. Part of my problem had been my elderly, sick mother whom I left at home with only a helper and my three-year-old grandson. There were days I returned home and spent the night with them; but it was strenuous as Matau is quite a journey from Phokeng. So at the end of the year I bade the school farewell.

*Kealeboga-grandson.*

*Keamogetswe-granddaughter.*

# Tlhabane College:
# Storm In A Teacup

◆

The buildings of Tlhabane College of Education were those used by Tlhabane Training School. Apart from the name, nothing was really new when I arrived there in 1983. A few more buildings were added here and there during my stay.

Although the institution had been upgraded to a college of Education, a lot still had to change.

The institution had managed to transfer a number of teachers who did not qualify as lecturers in a college of education; but a few still awaited their next appointments. When I arrived, there were two staff rooms, one for black lecturers and the other for whites; the same went for tearooms. There had been little if any integration of the staff of this institution; it had remained a racially divided college - except for the students who were all black.

The racial division in the education system of the past was peculiar. Black children were not allowed into white schools. White teachers, on the other hand, could not only staff a black institution; they were often paid extra for doing so. A question arises: could they honestly say they loved their black pupils when they would not share a staffroom or tearoom with their black counterparts?

Tlhabane College of Education when I arrived had a white rector, Mr Brian Podesta, and a number of Afrikaner lecturers of inferior qualifications, but holding senior positions. While black staff members had been transferred because of inferior qualifications; white lecturers on the other hand, were left in their posts. Their salaries exceeded ours and they received something extra for leaving town and coming to work in a black area.

The South Africa ambassador to Bophuthatswana would visit the white staff from time to time. During such days when they met with their ambassador, the rest of us would be invited to attend; if we wanted to. It was a fruitless exercise however. These encounters were conducted in such sophisticated Afrikaans that we Blacks were left in the dark. We could not understand anything. We therefore abandoned these meetings through sheer frustration.

There were some English speakers on the staff. One was Dr. Gordon Bauer, a philosopher who never tired of challenging staff and students to think and think critically. Mrs. Helen Metcalf, Mrs Daphne Hamilton, Mr. Dave Dalton, and Ms Pat Scott, Ms Tracy Kaplan, and Mr and Mrs. Mathews - all of them versatile and creative, completed the English-speaking component. There were also Bro Finbarr Murphy and Bro Lawrence Broderick who headed Teaching Practice and Maths/Science, respectively. Because we blacks were mostly English inclined, we found it a pleasure sharing ideas with this group.

Mr and Mrs Matthews, with whom I became very friendly, had come to Rustenburg from Zambia. The husband has since died of cardiac problems and the wife still resides in Rustenburg. When the husband died, I was no longer at the college, but I was called upon to give a speech at his funeral. I saw him as a very good and honest man.

At our first staff meeting in 1983 where the majority of us were new, the issue of separate tea rooms arose. It was readily resolved to share the same staff facilities, and to start right away. This was a small but significant breakthrough. Realistically, it was a step towards greater integration and symbolically it pointed to greater possibilities.

Inevitably the rector, Mr Podesta, came under increasing black pressure as our demands mounted. Why were Whites being appointed to head departments while dedicated black lecturers with good track records were being overlooked? Regarding my own position, I was not only qualified to be at this institution but my track record spoke for itself. I had been principal of a high school for eight years and my work was outstanding. It therefore followed that I could make a worthwhile contribution to the mission of Tlhabane College of Education. Furthermore, my age was also right for this institution.

Despite all this I found the rector somewhat cautious in offering me a better post, and I asked myself what more proof of my professional competencies he needed. In due course however I was promoted to be head of African Studies.

The white staff was mostly Afrikaans-speaking and in my judgment; quite conservative. From time to time they would organise a tea party, from which we blacks felt excluded. They claimed that they used their own contributions. How could we be sure of that we asked ourselves? Most of us found them as permanent staff members at the college when we arrived. They were firmly in charge still because they were in control of the college funds. After all, those who pay the piper call the tune!

But we felt this tune would have to change; and the piper and paymaster would have to be replaced. A drastic change though is bound to miscarry. We had to allow space for a gradual transformation to take its course. It is the same in South Africa today, even after 12 years of democracy. We still complain of racism, of the poor becoming poorer, and of poor service provision especially in the remotest parts of the country.

But these whites-only tea parties had to be challenged. Matters came to a head one day. One elderly Afrikaner lady responded to a few of us quite innocently, and without meaning to hurt. But hurt she did. She exclaimed, "We don't invite you to our tea parties because some of your men folk when they find cakes on a plate never consider that other people must also get a share."

The allegation as we felt it at that moment was that we blacks take everything; that we had not appreciated the value of sharing. This was all nonsense. Black people have been a sharing nation from time immemorial. We shared almost anything.

Soon after this incident a meeting was convened and the Whites-only tea parties ceased. Thereafter, we all contributed towards the parties which in their way, helped to unite us. Bit by bit, communication improved and we were enabled to span boundaries of race, ethnicity, nationality, language, culture, competency, creed, and age.

Would such an incident occur in today's South Africa? Hardly. It would be dismissed as just a storm in a teacup. Any guy of whatever race, going too greedily for cakes would be quickly put in his place.

Mr Podesta deservedly enjoyed the respect of staff and students, and growth became the buzz word of the college. Things changed even more wonderfully with the appointment of the first black rector, Mr. Jonas Chadi. Here was a man we Blacks could easily identify with. He brought many progressive changes to the institution. Quiet-spoken and very diligent, he filled his post to perfection. I think the entire staff enjoyed his style of leadership. His spouse, quiet and diligent like himself, was a member of staff.

In my view, the college was going from strength, each rector building on the work of his predecessor and reflecting the gradually improving political climate of the nineteen-eighties. But neither Mr Podesta nor Mr Chadi would have had a position at all, without an institution called Tlhabane Teacher Training School which was founded by Mr Greyling. Each played their respective roles within the political restrictions of those challenging times.

Unfortunately for Mr Chadi, he encountered the same problems with his masters at head office, as I did when principal of Tshukudu High School. These head office authorities were always ready to cause the downfall of anyone who excelled and who was not one of them. He had so many problems that the tension and pressure caused him major health problems.

In the college, we also progressed to a multi-racial women's prayer group which included Mrs. Hanna Greyling whose husband was founder of the college. During break we would meet for about 20 minutes. One of us would have prepared a text which we shared applying it to our own personal lives. Then anyone who wished to, prayed. Not all female members of staff became part of these prayer meetings.

We taught students in three levels. One group specialized in early childhood development. These teachers would qualify to teach in crèches and pre-schools after three years. Another group studied for the three-year primary teachers' diploma. The last group focused on the secondary school teachers' diploma which was also a three-year course.

Apart from my work as head of the department I also volunteered to serve on the disciplinary committee, in the heads of department forum, on the language committee, and on the finance committee.

I taught with men and women who did not need supervision. We were in authority ourselves; we spoke out when someone was not prepared to tow the line.

In 1985 January, I was preparing to sit for the B.Ed. exam when I was suddenly taken ill, alone in the house. I vomited the whole way as I crawled with great difficulty to the phone, I failed to get my hands on it. It was placed too high up. Still vomiting I crawled back to my bedroom thinking only of the worst.

The catechist of our church in Phokeng, Rosina, was on her way to town to prepare for a funeral of the daughter of one of our parishioners. As a friend, she asked the driver, Dingaan, to take a turn at my house to inform me about this funeral. I could hear them knock on the front door but I could not respond. All the doors were open. When they entered through the kitchen door they were immediately led by the trail of vomit to the bedroom. The driver was immediately sent to call our parish priest, Father Hunt who did not waste anytime.

Before Father Hunt arrived, my former student Monty also came in, not knowing of the crisis I was in. As a member of the born-again Christians, he prayed for me and assured me that I would be all right. Father Hunt anointed me. At that stage I could not even utter the Act of Contrition, which is the usual confession prayer. The priest had to say it for me. This sacrament called the Anointing of the Sick has two important purposes: for the sick person to be healed, if that is God's will; or for the sick person to die peacefully having been cleansed of their sins.

I was driven to Ga-Rankuwa Hospital still vomiting and perspiring heavily. As is the case with government hospitals I had to wait in a queue to be x-rayed, though still in acute pain.

My eldest son, Kennedy, was in the sixth year at Medunsa (Medical University of South Africa). As a student doctor he was always around when my medical history was recorded. I answered questions where I could, but sometimes I would just black out. When I came to each time, I would ask for something that could kill the pain. Medical staff told me they had tried all the strong drugs available, but they could not minimize the pain. I was not to drink water. Night came, the pain worsened and I felt all alone in my misery.

I could hear the nurses who took up the morning shift asking whether that woman was still alive!

When doctors arrived they told me the x-rays were of little help to them, but in any case they were going to operate. By this time I did not care a bit what they did with me. I just needed relief from the pain. I could not even see the operation permission form I was required to sign. My son was not allowed by law to sign for me. To simplify matters, they asked him to hold my hand as I signed. Thus I granted them permission to operate.

They cut open my stomach, for that was where the pain originated. They found that I suffered from intestinal obstruction which caused profuse bleeding. This had also caused the vomiting. The obstructed part of the intestine was removed. The rejoining was done with plastic.

My sister Midah was sitting on the chair next to my bed waiting for me to wake up after the operation. She was pale with fright. That was the first time I lay sick in hospital apart from occasions of childbirth.

Some of my colleagues from Tlhabane College of Education, Br Finbarr Murphy, Mr and Mrs Matthews and others paid me a visit and brought me much relief to my pains.

But there was a problem. Instead of healing, the wound remained septic. I was discharged with dressings to clean the wound three times a day until it was completely healed. I had lost a tremendous amount of weight.

After three months I resumed work. I also sat for the B.Ed exams and passed. That was a real achievement.

*Maggie Adjudicate Speech Contest-Ndebele College Of Education.*

# People Power Or Pupil Power?

◆

When the National Party came to power in 1948 it set out to entrench white privilege, and quickly redesigned the education system. Afrikaans was placed on a par with English; white students would have to be proficient in both languages.

As a pupil completing my primary schooling, I feared the implications of the National Party's new plans for education. The Bantu Education Act of 1953, I was to learn later, widened the gap between blacks and whites. Separate schooling systems were established for blacks, whites, and coloureds. We black students knew we were getting a raw deal. Passing through white suburbs we would envy those spacious sports grounds and fine buildings and we could only guess as to the scale of their labs and libraries. We dare not step inside the gate because notices such as Slegs Blanke ('Whites Only) clearly warned us.

Whites were guaranteed quality education, and protected against competition from other race groups. The discrepancies in education among racial groups were glaring. Teacher-pupil ratios in white primary schools averaged 1:18; 1:24 in Asian schools; 1:27 in coloured schools and 1:39 in black schools. Moreover, whereas 96% of all teachers in white schools had teaching certificates, only 15 percent of teachers in black schools were certificated. Secondary school pass rates for black pupils in the nationwide, standardised high school graduation examinations were less than one-half the pass rate for whites. Behind these figures lies the painful reality of poverty and deprivation that marked our secondary schools. Student-teacher ratio could run to 1:60 and more. Labs and libraries, if they existed at all, were poorly equipped. What would attract a black BA graduate to apply for a teaching post in such an environment?

With dismay we noted the rising political tensions throughout the 1960s. Internal security laws grew ever more repressive, and the period of detention without trial was extended ever further. Pretoria was obsessed with the dangers posed by Communism.

Racial segregation, imposed by the Group Areas Act, was reducing us to the level of paupers and beggars in our own country. We blacks were denied the right to settle where we wanted, and commuting to work involved pre-dawn travel. We were cheated out of our right to vote for a meaningful representative government. We had long since lost our lands. Our war veterans, returning from World War 2 had been awarded bicycles, instead of farms; our women had lost the battle against the pass laws. Now to crown it all, our access to quality education was severely hampered. In our African primary schools, the medium of instruction was no longer English, but mother tongue. The church and missionaries had been sidelined and silenced, including some outstanding Catholic schools. In fact the Catholic Church was branded by Pretoria as die Romse gevaar ( the Roman danger); this would distinguish it from the Communist Party, labelled die Rooi gevaar ( the Red danger)

But all was well, the state broadcaster assured South Africans, because the Bantu Education Act was looking after the Bantu child. And the National Party proposed this grand design for independent African homelands where Black leaders would develop their people "along their own lines". Wasn't this the core concept labelled apartheid, separate development? This is how the National Party propaganda machine disguised its own greed, and tried to trick the black majority into believing that the emerging Bantustans were truly the "Promised Land".

The saying goes: "You can fool some of the people all the time, and all the people some of the time, but you cannot fool all the people all the time!"

For two centuries education remained an ever-contested issue, first between Brits and Boers, but now in the 1970s, it urgently engaged the black majority. They were deprived, and in many cases desperate. One of the central curricular issues in education was the medium of instruction. Afrikaans was enforced by the National Party as the medium of instruction for half the subjects offered in black secondary schools. But as the Afrikaner resisted the English language and most of what it stood for, so the blacks were resisting Afrikaans.

Repeated complaints from the Soweto schools in the early months of 1976 went unheeded. Indeed the Minister for the Department of Native Affairs was alleged to have retorted that if the students weren't happy with Afrikaans, then they didn't have to come to school at all! The eruption of June 16 is now history. Afrikaans proved to be the straw that broke the camel's back. But whose back? That of the National Party of course! The struggle for liberation had passed to tens of thousands of black youth, never again to be cowed by anybody, white or black.

Investment per capita in the white student was about ten times that of his/her black counterpart.

In the 1970s I now witnessed these deprivations from another angle, as an educator, and as a mother.

Many young people during the 1980s were committed to destroying the school system because of its identification with apartheid. Student strikes, vandalism, and violence seriously undermined the school's ability to function. By the early 1990s, shortages of teachers, classrooms, and equipment had taken a further toll on education.

The National Party was able to capitalise on the fear of racial integration in the schools to build its support. The National Party's narrow election victory in 1948 gave Afrikaners new standing in the schools. After that, all high schools graduates were required to be proficient in both Afrikaans and English. The National Party further re-introduced Christian National Education as the guiding philosophy of education.

Schools in South Africa, as elsewhere, reflect society's political philosophy and goals. The earliest mission schools aimed to inculcate literacy and new social and religious values. Schools for European immigrants aimed to preserve the values of previous generations. In the 20th century, the education system assumed economic importance as it prepared young Africans for low wage labour and protected the privileged white minority from competition. From the 1950s to the mid 1990s, social institutions reflected the government's racial philosophy of apartheid more clearly than did the education system. Because the schools were required to teach and to practice apartheid, they were especially vulnerable to the weaknesses of the system.

The Bantu Education Act (No. 47) of 1953 widened the gap in education opportunities for different racial groups. Two of the architects of Bantu

Education, Dr. W. M. Eiselen and Dr. Hendrick F. Verwoerd had studied in Germany. They had adopted many elements of National Socialist (Nazi) philosophy. The concept of racial purity in particular, provided a rationalization for keeping black education inferior. It said black Africans should be educated for their opportunities in life and that there was no place for them "above the level of certain forms of labour". Later he explained to senate: "So what is the use of teaching the Bantu child mathematics when he cannot use it in practice?"

Following the Eiselen Report (1951), black education was removed from missionary control to the Native Affairs Department. As Verwoerd put it: "I will reform it (black education) so that the Natives will be taught from childhood to realise that equality with Europeans is not for them."
Widespread boycotts by pupils and teachers erupted the day that Bantu Education came into effect. Seven thousand pupils and 116 teachers were dismissed.

The Extension of University Education Act of 1957 closed undergraduate classes at white universities. Colleges were created to take University of South Africa degrees and diplomas. In addition to Fort Hare, which was now reserved for the Xhosa, new colleges were opened at Turfloop, (Sotho, Venda and Nguni), hence also known as SOVENGA; Durban Westville (Indian), Cape Town Bellville, (Coloured) and Ngoye (Zulu) in Zululand. After many protests, the Act came into force in 1959. Many lecturers at Fort Hare resigned, including its African vice-principal Z.K. Matthews. Within a few years, only one or two of the original lecturers remained. The five non-white colleges were in future staffed largely by Afrikaans-speaking whites.

Verwoerd recognised that expanding industries in "white areas" needed an expanding black labour force. But he predicted that the black urban population would begin to fall in the late 1970s, by which time apartheid would have succeeded in developing the black rural reserves as alternative areas of employment. Verwoerd saw total separation between white and black societies as the final aim of apartheid. Black labour in white society was like "donkeys, oxen and tractors", which could someday be replaced by other machinery.

Because of the government's "homeland" policy, no new high schools were built in Soweto between 1962 and 1971. Students were meant to move to their relevant homelands to attend newly built schools there. Then in 1972 the government gave in to pressure from business to improve the Bantu Education system to meet business needs for a better-trained black workforce. Forty more schools were built in Soweto. Between 1972 and 1976 the number of pupils at secondary schools increased from 12 656 to 34 656. One in five Soweto children was attending secondary school.

Tension over the medium of instruction erupted into violence on June 16, 1976. Students took to the streets in the Johannesburg township of Soweto. Their action was prompted by the previous decision of Prime Minister Hendrick Verwoerd to enforce a regulation requiring that one-half of all high-school subjects be taught in Afrikaans. A harsh police response resulted in the deaths of several children, some as young as eight or nine years. In the violence that followed, 575 people died, and at least 134 of them were under the age of 18.

Youthful ANC supporters abandoned school in droves, some vowing to "make South Africa ungovernable," in protest against apartheid. Others left the country for military training camps run by the ANC or other liberation armies, mostly in Angola, Tanzania or Eastern Europe. "Liberation before education" became their battle cry.

Schools suffered further damage as a result of the unrest of 1976. Vandals and arsonists damaged or destroyed many schools and public properties. Students and teachers who tried to attend school were attacked. Some teachers and administrators joined in the protests.

The National Policy for General Affairs Act (No. 76) of 1984 provided some improvements in black education but maintained the overall separation called for by the Bantu Education system. This Act gave the Minister of National Education authority to determine general policy for syllabuses, examinations and certificate qualifications in all institutions of formal education. However, responsibility for implementing these policies was divided among numerous government departments and offices, resulting in a bewildering array of educational authorities. Thus, the Department of Education and Training was responsible for black education outside the homelands. Each of the three houses of parliament - for whites, coloureds, and Indians  administered education for each racial group. Add to these the ten homelands, each with its own education department. In addition, several other government departments managed specific aspects of education.

Education was compulsory for all racial groups, but at different ages, and the law was enforced differently and unevenly. Whites were required to attend school between the ages of seven and 16. Black children were required to enrol from age seven until the equivalent of seventh grade or the age of 16. But this law was badly enforced, and not at all in areas where schools were unavailable. For Asians and coloureds, education was compulsory between the ages of seven and 15.

As the government implemented the 1984 legislation, fresh violence flared up in response to the limited constitutional reforms that continued to exclude blacks.

The Soweto riots of 1976 were not to be confined to Soweto only. Many other schools outside this area joined in. Boarding schools, tertiary institutions, rural and semi-rural schools were equally affected.

My son, Kennedy, was at Hebron Secondary School in 1977 doing Grade 10 (what was then Form III). A resident student, he was in Standard Nine in 1978, which was also known as Form IV or present Grade 11.

As parents with children in distant boarding schools, we were always glued to radio and TV. When riots broke out in one school, we knew that the next school would be affected. We could expect to see our children arriving home at any time during the school year. Then after some weeks schools would re-open and students would return - but only until the next strike which could be a matter of weeks, or even days! It was a vicious circle.

My husband, Solly, and myself finally got tired of these comings and goings and enrolled our son locally in Bafokeng High School. He stayed at this school until he passed Matric with very good symbols in 1979.

In those days when a student wanted to pursue a career in medicine, they had to do a pre-medical course for a year; then they would go to a medical school to start the second year.

Kennedy attended the University of the North for a year. This course was reputed to be very difficult. Afrikaner lecturers would warn students: "I expect only five of you to pass at the end of the year." This warning was issued even before formal lectures began. The lecture halls were full to capacity, but you can imagine the morale of the students on hearing such a negative message, which was really a prophecy of doom. Such prophecies are all too often self-fulfilling!

The same vicious circle of riots that marked secondary education, established itself in tertiary institutions as well, and with the inevitable pattern of disruption. How many times did Kennedy have to trek back and forth to the

University of the North that one year? However, all ended with success. He entered the Medical University of Southern Africa (Medunsa), to do his second year in medicine in 1981.

The rioting at Medunsa was even worse than that of the north! Medunsa is next to Ga-Rankuwa Hospital where the medical students practised. The university and hospital were situated on the sensitive border between the Republic of South Africa and Bophuthatswana. They were deemed to be resident in Pretoria while the township of Ga-Rankuwa was in Bophuthatswana.

During riots, police from Pretoria would charge into the campus and assault students clearing them out of the premises. In their confusion, students would leap across the fence, and find themselves in Ga-Rankuwa, which was part of Bophuthatswana. There they found the homeland police ready to receive them. They would also assault the students taunting them to return to South Africa, and not to cause trouble in their territory. It was a case of jumping from the frying pan into the fire!

One afternoon I was in Rustenburg doing some shopping in Checkers Supermarket. I had just come out of Tlhabane College where I was a lecturer. A neighbour of mine from Phokeng informed me that she had spotted my son surrounded by police. At this stage Kennedy was using one of the family cars. He was on his way to urgently fetch something from home.

The police were attracted by the AZAPO sticker on his car and stopped him. When they searched the vehicle, they found AZAPO documents and a T-Shirt. While his car was parked at the Rustenburg Police Station, Special Branch members took him for questioning.

I immediately abandoned the groceries at the counter without paying for them and rushed to the police station, only to be directed to the Special Branch. When I arrived there, I demanded to know what Kennedy's offence was supposed to be. The response was typically blunt, "Wait outside while we question him." I waited for what seemed to be an eternity.

He was immediately identified as one of the executive members of the Azanian People's Organisation, (AZAPO) and as having a brother studying in America! He was asked why Harold had to go to the United States when there were enough universities in South Africa. Why had he left the University of Cape Town before completing his degree there? These and many other irrelevant questions Kennedy had to respond to.

After his interrogation he was set free, but with threats that he was under surveillance.

His second brush with the police was at the village of Tlokweng (Silverkrans) about 80km north west of Rustenburg. A number of Medunsa students went there to attend the wedding celebrations of a classmate. Students being students, they started making political remarks and chanting slogans. The police were called, and the students continued their celebrations in the cells of the Madikoe police station for the rest of that weekend!

When I was in police custody in 1988, one of my constant worries was Kennedy's relations with the homeland police. During interrogation, I was warned that my children would also be taken into custody. That was an instruction "from above". Of course Kennedy flouted the rules every time he visited me in prison, but that was the risk he faced as a devoted son.

Harold visited me in Rooigrond when he was home on holidays. To him the whole struggle in Bop was just a fiasco; it made little sense to him. Fortunately his stay in the country was brief and he slipped quietly back to the United States. I was relieved that at least one of my boys was beyond the reach of the Bop police.

The black children of South Africa had taken up the war against Bantu Education generally, and Afrikaans as a medium of instruction, in particular. What about their parents? Parents made their voices heard only when it was too late and many children had been imprisoned and tortured, or had died at the hands of the South African police. If parents had played their proper part in the struggle, things would have been different.

In their absence, students seized control, and "called the shots". The slogans, "Injury to one is injury to all" and "Pass one, pass all", speak for themselves. In many schools, uniforms were discarded altogether. Teachers lost control. Students chased principals or teachers off the premises to make them "tow the line"; but whose line? Law and order had been replaced by mob rule.

Other authority structures such as the prefect system were challenged to their foundations. Prefects were replaced by student representative councils (SRCs). These bodies yielded raw power in secondary and tertiary institutions. In a new form of tyranny, memoranda were drafted by semi-illiterate students or pupils. Demands were then put to the authorities and little scope was allowed for effective consultation and negotiation. Was this people's power, or pupils' power?

Finally, the government began to signal its awareness that apartheid could not endure. By 1986, President P. W. Botha (1984-1989) had stated that the concept of apartheid was "outdated" and behind-the-scenes negotiations had begun between government officials and imprisoned ANC leader Nelson Mandela. The gap between governments spending on education for different racial groups slowly began to narrow, and penalties for defying apartheid rules in education began to ease.

The 1976 riots should be a reminder for all parents. Parents must be actively involved in their children's education. If they fail to carry out this simple task, children will take matters into their own hands, and with disastrous consequences.

When children started parroting "Liberation now, education later" many adults were not aware of the consequences. Later these children, who were deprived of education, grew up to become deprived young men and women. Then society came round and labelled them "the lost generation". How did they get lost when parents had been there all along?

If we look back to the previous generation we might ask why parents ever allowed the apartheid regime to rule - or misrule - the country as it did. Before rushing to condemn these parents, please remember the quality of Bantu education they themselves had experienced. After all, Verwoerd had ruled in the early 1950s that black pupils should be prepared mainly for lives of manual labour. Blacks had never been permitted to participate meaningfully in the national political discourse. What did they know about their human and civil rights? Zero! But was it their fault? They were trapped in their Bantustans.

It is no great surprise therefore that the irresponsible slogan about liberation first and education later, went largely unnoticed. We might also ask in passing, who were the authors and protagonists of this vicious campaign which misled tens of thousands of our young people. Did some emerging black leaders of the mid-1980s conspire with it, and go on to occupy high positions in our country today. At any rate, the new government has inherited the lost generation with all its incipient problems of unemployment, illiteracy, lack of housing, poverty, homelessness, and many other societal ills.

*Lebone grandson.*

*Kennedy my eldest son.*

# The Status Of Teachers

◆

During my time as a primary schoolgirl, teachers had their houses in the schoolyard. Communities built these houses. In the case of Polonia, the church provided for the houses. During manual work we not only cleaned the houses, but washed pots and dishes. Sometimes we even cooked the teachers' meals and did the washing.

At Moiletswane my grandparents' house was just next to the school. Whenever teachers needed assistance they came to grandma. They were regularly supplied with milk, which they always waited for at the kraal during milking times. Over weekends, they often went away and asked that I remain in the house with their children.

There was one principal, Mr Mothibe, and his wife. They were newly married and when they started a family sometimes their baby would be left with grandma. I was always involved with helping grandma look after the baby. Later when the family increased, a girl called Rina, a relative of Mrs. Mothibe came to live with them. On days when the couple moved out, I would be called upon to keep her company in the house.

Then there was a lady teacher who was accommodated next to the principal's house. She came to Moiletswane with two girls, her nieces who were my age. Their aunt always left on Friday afternoon and returned on Sunday evening. During such days, two or three of us would sleep together with these girls, keeping them company.

Teachers back then spent very little money. Teachers did not have to pay for any services rendered to them. In fact communities felt duty bound to receive them among their midst with warmth. They offered to give any assistance required. Teachers did not have to pay for it. The community took them as people who had come as a favour, to teach their children. They were handled with great respect.

Not only did we clean the teachers' homes and prepare their meals we took turns providing them with tasty dishes. The mothers baked for them and when it was time for mielies, they cooked them and gave them to our teachers. There was a certain type of sweet potato, which we always ate at Moiletswane. I am surprised that I cannot find them today. We cooked them in the evening with a little water, added a little salt to taste, and left them to cool for the night. In the morning we enjoyed them with black tea. They were sweet and hard. During such times, our teachers always had some.

They were invited to weddings and all parties. Afterwards they would be sent home with food parcels. Of course they also behaved as part of the communities they served, not as strangers. They attended all community gatherings. They went to funerals and attended kgotla. When there was any translation to be done for the community, they were ready to help. They went to churches and offered their services as required.

There was never a question of "us and them" as it is the case today. Some of them came from far but still were respected by communities.

My Grade Two teacher Miss Kate Rametsi at Polonia left shortly after I commenced Grade Two. She loved me very much, and I loved her too. She appreciated my achievement in class. The community also loved her. She was so special. Miss Rametsi came from the Northern Transvaal Soekmekaar. She was to get married to a man at home and had to leave Polonia School to return home for the wedding and settle there. The school and the community showered her with presents. A car came to fetch her one morning. The driver of the car had to be slow as the whole community and the school walked on both sides and behind. Some women were ululating as a sign she was going to get married. We children were crying to lose such a teacher. I had wanted throughout my lifetime to meet this special person, to hug her and to tell her my life stories. I cannot even recall whom she was marrying. This would perhaps make it easier for me to trace her. Her first name was Kate. If Kate is still alive she must be very old now. At the time she left Polonia she was very young. She could have been in her mid 20s. She was not only a kind teacher. She was also very beautiful and had a special way of dressing.

Then there was a teacher at Moiletswane who also appreciated my work very much. When I left Moiletswane at the end of 1951, Mr. Tshetlo gave me a present. It was a small English Dictionary. Inside he had written, "Present to Maggie Chengwe, from her loving teacher, S.S. Tshetlo." I had never used a dictionary before. That was my first dictionary. When I got to Standard Four in Polonia, my classmates saw this "new girl" with an English Dictionary. They realised then that this must be a special girl. My new class teacher, Mr Phillip Mahuma, also realised this. He asked if he could look at my dictionary. He looked into it, looked at me and after a few questions, trying to know me better, he gave it back.

I made good use of this dictionary. Mr. Mahuma was to realise later that I was not just one of his scholars. I was an achiever and I proved it from the beginning. He said now and again that he would like to meet the parents of this bright scholar. He did visit my home and met my mother and told her in no uncertain terms how bright a scholar I was and that my parents are faced with the challenge of educating me.

One of my maternal uncles, Robinson, worked in a shop in De Wildt. Whenever I was sent on errands I'd make sure to go to that particular shop to meet him. He loved to see me now and then. When I came in he'd shout at the top of his voice: "Setlogolo! Come to uncle!" He would then give me sweets and some food parcels for his sister, my mother. One day I happened to be there at the same time with the principal of our school. In my presence the principal was commenting to my uncle about the wonderful niece the family had produced; what a promising scholar I was, while pleading with my uncle to assist in my future education. Maybe it is my nature, or the nature of the children of those days, or perhaps it was also because of my humble background that I never became too excited by such praise. In some way, knowing my family's poverty I always wondered whether I'd really make it to the top, academically. I wanted to, so much. My determination must have come, partly at least, from mom's optimism.

The highlights of our primary school days were the school trips. We visited the zoos in Pretoria. We would also go to the museum, to the mint, and sometimes we visited the aerodromes. We went to play basketball and soccer with another school or they came to us. We went to music competitions. We always looked forward to winning. I was not an athlete but I played basketball. I also sang in the choir. We had our own choir where we sang in school concerts. When we were selected to sing in the choir, a candle was lit and you had to sing while it was burning. The trick was you should not exhale in such a way as to extinguish the candle. This test was performed by our class-teacher, Mr. Mahuma on my arrival at Polonia from Moiletswane. I performed in front of the candle, it continued to burn, and so I was admitted to the choir immediately. It was here that my confidence in singing was built. I realised then that I could sing, and started to love it. I occasionally sang a duet with a girl called Margaret, at church festivals or in school choirs. Church and school were one. The school sang at all the church celebrations.

When I was at Moiletswane, I could not sing. I just moved my lips producing no sound. My teacher, Mr. Tshetlo called me one day and reprimanding me, challenged: "How can you a bright scholar do this to me? I realise you just move your lips." He was disappointed in me. I could not hold my place in the choir. The school concerts often held at night were the worst. Sometimes I would fall asleep while standing in a choir in front of the audience and had to be continuously woken up! For some reason, I was unaware of my musical talent until I got to Polonia in 1952. My grandma was shocked when I was at times, excluded from the choir.

When going on school trips, we made thorough preparations regarding refreshments for the day. A chicken was prepared and cooked. Sour porridge was prepared. We also carried fat cakes and tea in bottles. Then our clothes (black and white) had to be particularly neat and ironed. We would take a bath and wake up very early for the trips. Friends always ate together. We also carried some pocket money for luxuries like ice cream and cold drinks. Our teachers never carried food. We were glad to provide them with a share from our own provisions.

There was a school called Rooistad Primary where the present Zone 3 Ga-Rankuwa now stands. We always looked forward to play this school where they spoke isi-Tsonga. After they left we would have picked up a few new words. As we played, the food would be laid under the trees. Anybody could go and have a bite when they felt hungry. One day, a pig took one of the food packets. One of the kids kept shouting to the owner ingolobe itekile boswa ("the pig has grabbed your bread"). There was quite a commotion chasing that pig, but we failed to corner it. Later the food was dropped somewhere but it was too unclean for human consumption. The other kids kindly shared their food with this unfortunate boy.

In those days we had no sports attire. We wore our own pants when playing basketball. They were of different patterns and colours. As I visited my mum at her place of work I also helped her with the duties assigned her. But at times I was offered jobs, such as supervising the kids at play, to make my own pocket money. Before working at Foresttown, mom was employed at Craighall Park by a couple who were both medical doctors at Baragwanath Hospital. One holiday they asked mom to send me over for a piece job. When mom left them, it was negotiated that she would find a lighter job. She was ill most of the time, sometimes vomiting blood.

They got her a job with their friends at Foresttown. She enjoyed a very good working relationship with her employers. While I held a holiday job with them, I played with and fed the kids. At the end of my holidays, besides payments the lady would open her wardrobe and ask me to select whatever I wanted. One of the items I chose was a slack dress. The top was a dress; the lower part was a short slack, blue in colour. I loved it. I was going to use it as my basketball attire.

Our mode of transport for our school trips for many years was an open truck. Later the trucks were closed. Only years later did we become so sophisticated that we used buses. We never went on school trips without the accompaniment of adults. Even in their absence we were just children. In the company of boys or not, it made no difference. We played together, we swam together, and we fetched water together. There was never a feeling of any difference between us. Today it is uncommon for boys and girls to be just plutonic friends. When I think of it now I realise how very light the work of a teacher was in those days. Going on school trips today is a real hassle, never pleasant for teachers and parents.

Teachers were respected and were law that was accepted by communities. I remember one day when my cousin, Kgogo, was to be punished at school in Moiletswane. He escaped and ran away. The boys and the teacher ran after him. But he was too fast. He climbed the hill at the end of the village. They called it Mallaphiri ("where the wolves cry"). The group lost him and had to return without him. However, they came to grandma and reported their problem. They must have agreed with her about their next move. I did not know this. Perhaps I was not to be told, as we were very close to each other. In fact, his 'crime' was that he had beaten a lad who had pushed me!

I did not see or hear him come home that night. All that I know is that while I was preparing to go to school the next day, the teacher arrived accompanied by the same boys that chased and lost him the previous day. Poor cousin Kgogo! He was still fast asleep, apparently exhausted from the ordeal of yesterday. When he woke up he must have been planning to escape to the hill again and avoid school and punishment. But the teacher was too fast. When he woke up, the same people who had been baying for his blood the previous day surrounded him at his bed. They got hold of him, dragged him to school where he was thoroughly beaten with a seasoned rod.

Kgogo was so angry that he felt like quitting school forever, but that was not to be. Grandma and the teacher would not allow him do as he pleased. So back to school he went. I pitied him and definitely I wanted him back. Whenever they discussed his 'crime' I felt extremely annoyed. But I suppose that was part of my growing up.

Our primary schools, unlike schools today, were surrounded by bare ground. In some cases you'd find trees as in Polonia, which were planted by German missionaries. There were no flower gardens. On Fridays during manual work, we scrubbed the cement floors and washed the windows. Outside the classrooms, we swept the space clean with our homemade brooms, or just branches of trees. For polish we brought candles, melted them, and when the wax was cold we added paraffin. We called the mixture waskers.

At Moiletswane, on the other hand, the classroom floors were of mud, not cement. When it was cleaning time we used cow dung from our home kraals. This we mixed with water and applied it to the floor. Girls designed different patterns they had learned at home to make classroom floors look beautiful. This was the same stuff we used in our lapa, the courtyard at home. Once a year, the floors had to be renewed. To do this mothers would take soil mixed with dung, and spread it on the floor, making a good layer. Then they would smooth the floor with a stone called thitelo. It would be allowed to dry for a day or two. After this, cow dung was used to give the floor the finishing touch. There were people who excelled in this craft. Even if it rained the soil would hold because of the dung.

The walls of our courtyards at home, and even schools, were renewed annually in this manner. For the walls cow dung was not used as a finish. The smoothing stone was not used either. Instead, mothers used their hands to make the walls smooth and even. It was not difficult to obtain cow dung. We could just follow the cattle as they grazed and pick up fresh dung. You must understand that farmers were very strict about allowing a person to enter their kraals.

Boys repaired broken window panes. They also carried soil to fill up potholes caused by rainwater. They did repair jobs and handiwork while girls did needle work. I happened to be very poor in needlework. We produced a variety of useful articles such as children's dresses, bibs, aprons and girls' skirts. We used our hands as no sewing machines were available to us. The articles made from needlework and the boys' handiwork were sold to the public.

I always wondered why I could not sew. My mother had a sewing machine, which she used to sew our dresses and her aprons. My eldest sister, Suzan, was an expert dressmaker. Even today my mother's sewing machine is still there. But it is old and it is not easy to get its missing parts, as new machines have come on the market now.

*Olivia Magae daughter.*

Part Five

# Political
# Consciousness
# And Activism
# Night Time

# Cry For Land

◆

B efore coming to Moiletswane, my maternal grandparents lived at a place called Monyamane. Monyamane was near Pretoria. The present new suburbs in Pretoria are situated in what was formally Monyamane. The suburb directly occupying the area is Doornpoort. Opposite is another rich suburb called Montana. Some of my cousins now live in these suburbs, but I wonder if they can reconcile these areas with who they are.

Moiletswane was actually bought by my maternal great-grandfather, Mamanare Solomon Motiang. Therefore the land that Grandfather, Lazarus Motiang and others fought so much for, was the land of their fathers. This information is contained and confirmed by the documents from the Department of Land Affairs. We, his great-grandchildren, learned about this only when we attended meetings to reclaim this land. On the list of buyers, names of children follow. The name Lazarus thus comes immediately under that of his father. It also stands to reason that Lazarus must have been the first-born in his family. His siblings' names and those of their children come after his name, and so on.

Moiletswane, a farm that is known in official documents as Elandsfontein 44OJQ, was bought in 1925. The present sub-chief, Mr. Matholo Phineas Motsepe, was able to lead the community in its efforts at obtaining all relevant information about the farm. He was assisted by an interim committee representing all the clans in the community.

Each household contributed a sum of £21 to purchase this farm.

As in my family, the farm was paid for by our great-grandfather, Mamanare. The names of his three sons, Lazarus Manyarela Motiang, Shadrack Matia

Motiang, and Morake Daniel Motiang appear in the list of purchasers, under Mamanare. In all there are 94 names on that list.

Ironically, no female name appears. Yet there were daughters in these households.

The traditional trend at that time was that girls were excluded as heirs to their parents' inheritance. On the other hand, boys became heads of families at the death of their fathers, even if their mothers were still alive. This tradition has been changed by the "equality clause" in the new Constitution of South Africa. While our great-grandparents were already practising Christianity and could read the Bible, Galatians 3, 26-29 had obviously eluded them:

"For in Christ Jesus you are all children of God through faith. As many of you as were baptized into Christ have clothed yourselves with Christ. There is no longer Jew or Greek, there is no longer slave or free, there is no longer male and female; for all of you are one in Christ Jesus. And if you belong to Christ, then you are Abraham's offspring, heirs according to the promise."

I discovered later from original documents that the people of Moiletswane first came from different areas to settle on the farm, Elandsfontein 440JQ on the 15th October, 1875. It was only in 1925 that the community bought this farm. In 1961 they again bought this farm. In 1961 they purchased another piece of land, which includes a large part of the town of Brits.

Although the community was made to belong to the Mmakau chieftaincy by the laws of the time, none from outside the 94 clans mentioned here assisted in the purchase of the said farms. Not even the chief of the Mmakau tribe contributed anything towards the purchasing of their farm. It was unfortunate however, that the Mmakau chieftaincy was instrumental in the forceful removal of the community from farms which were lawfully theirs. It is also little wonder that today this community does not want to be associated with Mmakau, or to be referred to as Bakgatla-Ba-Mmakau. They prefer the name Bakgatla-Ba-Moiletswane.

In my view, the foresight of this community, their courage and their determination, are amazing. They are united forces who are prepared to live or die for what lawfully belongs to them. Like their forefathers, they do not easily give up.

My mother was born in 1910 at Monyamane. She was the first-born child in the family of six. The family left in 1916 when she was six years old. They were a large community and were staying on a farm owned by an Afrikaner. As is the case in the history of South Africa, there is always conflict between farm owners and tenants. It would appear that there was misunderstanding between the community and the Afrikaner, and this caused their departure. When my grandparents left to settle at Moiletswane, on a farm that their father had bought together with others, they left a certain section of the community at Monyamane. Up to 1954 there were still some of the family members living there. Later, the rest of the people were forced to resettle elsewhere. They dispersed. Some went to a place called Stinkwater, while others resettled in townships. The majority, however, are still at Moiletswane from where they were forcefully removed later. They resettled in a barren area near Dipompong, but the people still regard themselves as part of the Moiletswane community. They want to regain their independence and identity.

Today, as I write this book, I'm glad to inform you that we have secured the Title Deeds. More about this later. All the necessary procedures have been followed to verify all beneficiaries. We attend meetings once a month to put everything in place and to discuss the way forward. We have filled in claim forms, indicating grandpa's number, which identifies all his beneficiaries and their children. Platinum and other minerals have been discovered on this farm; discussions are going on about a company that will be allowed to do the mining. We also prepare to start a trust fund that will provide bursaries for children of beneficiaries. The first time I attended one of these meetings, I was fit to cry. Moiletswane was coming back to life again. Old neighbours and friends and former classmates were re-connecting. What a touching moment!

I was living in Polonia when I started school in 1947. After passing Standard One in 1949, I went to Moiletswane to assist my maternal grandparents. When I passed Standard Three in 1951, I returned to Polonia, and completed Standards Four and Five. Then I was asked to stay with my maternal uncle who was a teacher at Lehurutshe (Zeerust), in a village called Dinokana. There I became one of the best pupils in Standard Six in 1954. No pupil in class could beat me in arithmetic.

Every Friday we wrote a test in arithmetic and my name was always top of the list. Results were put on the door outside for all and sundry to see. My uncle was not fully aware of my potential when I first came to stay with him. The Friday results on the door amazed him.

At the end of the year, during the oral examinations, I represented the class in Afrikaans. I still recall being requested to relate a story of my own; this I did. It told of a man who had married two wives, one of whom was not reliable. The man caught a hare and asked the older woman to have it cooked. When she went to check the meat before serving it to her husband, there was none to be seen.

In my story in Afrikaans I said; "Toe die ouer vrou die pot oopmaak het sy gevind geen vleis."

The Afrikaner inspector testing me, probed, "Toe sy die pot oopmaak toe was die pot…" and I quickly replied: "Toe was die pot leeg".

The inspector was so impressed that he stopped his questions there and then. He enquired where I had come from and I replied: "Near Pretoria, Sir". He said that explained my fluency.

Usually teachers would meet to discuss oral examination results. Our teacher stated to the class that my proficiency in Afrikaans had saved them all.

Because of the proximity to Botswana, the Mafikeng and Lehurutshe areas were weak in Afrikaans. Even our class teacher, Ferdinand Moroeng, struggled with the language. His English however, was incredibly good. The local kgosi (chief), Ramotswere Moiloa, had attended school at the famed Lovedale College in the Eastern Cape together with our Standard Six teacher. Sometimes when we as a school visited the kgotla in Dinokana, the chief would address us in sophisticated English. He would allow our teacher to translate because the latter was also a product of Lovedale.

Leherutshe was soon to make national headlines, rural and remote though it was, when its women under the leadership of Gertrude Mphekwa united in their protest against the Pass Laws. Schools were closed, teachers sympathetic to the women's cause were transferred far and wide, and the women who had organized the resistance were carted off to prison in Zeerust. To crown it all, Kgosi Moiloa was exiled to Botswana. In the meantime, the house of the school principal had been torched.

# Branded Inferior

◆

At the national level another event concerned mainly with youth this time was unfolding. Rumours abounded about the primary school certificates being awarded by the newly established Department of Bantu Education. Why must we Standard Six pupils have the dubious honour of being first to earn these certificates? But then we reasoned, someone must be first, so why fret? But fret we did, but only as time allowed. Remember, we were caught up in revision work. Something else, our teachers, parents and adults generally were deafeningly silent about this new Department of Bantu Education and its new certificates.

Despite my youth - I was only 14 - this thing called Bantu Education was giving me sleepless nights. All along, I had felt in my deepest being that something was terribly unjust in our country. And here was the ultimate proof. Think of the armies of South African youths so keen on education, so full of laudable ambition, being served with the new certificate.

This certificate was a piece of paper that would brand us, the black majority, as inferior. After all, Bantu Education was designed to train the Bantu child for certain levels of manual labour, declared Prime Minister Verwoerd. Subsidies to church schools and colleges were withdrawn because they were "misleading" black students into believing that they could aspire to equality with whites So the new certificate was as much a statement of black inferiority as of academic achievement. At best it would admit a tiny number of us to mediocre institutions and bush universities. The future looked bleak indeed. And I asked myself how the National Party could stoop so low as to deprive us of our legitimate youthful hopes.

We saw many black professionals quit the schools rather than administer the poisonous system called Bantu Education. They fled the country, and then the apartheid authorities labelled them terrorists and communists. Denied access to the pen, little wonder some of these exiles turned to the sword.

I passed Standard Six with distinction in 1954. We primary school pupils were sad indeed. We knew that our problems in education had only just started. At the beginning of the following year we all scattered in different directions. Some were lucky to access the last few remaining institutions of note; others had to take what was left.

*Maggie and husband Solomon with baby Kennedy.*

# 'Independent' Dependent Bophuthatswana

◆

The groundwork for the implementation of Bantustans was laid after the 1948 victory of the National Party. The Population Registration Act of 1959 was passed which divided the South African population into white, black and coloured. The coloured group was further divided into Indian people and those of mixed racial descent. This Act was followed by the promotion of the Bantu Self-determination Act and the Group Areas Act. These Acts achieved the spatial separation of races and the white domination of African, Coloured and Indian people. The government feared any inclusion of these races on the basis of minority rule. Thus, the Bantu Self-determination Act served the purpose of justifying the continued exclusion of black people from incorporation into the South African parliamentary system.

Initially, ten Bantustans were established, namely, KwaZulu, Lebowa, Gazankulu, Qwaqwa, KaNgwane, KwaNdebele, Transkei, Bophuthatswana, Venda and Ciskei. All these Bantustans were in line with the ethnic background of each area.

Between 1976 and 1981, the South African government tried to force the Bantustans to accept independence from South Africa as separate black states. In 1977, Prime Minister John Vorster met Bantustan leaders. He promised them economic and political independence and the establishment of their own military.

In the same year, the Riekert Commission was set up to explore the feasibility of independent Bantustans. The commission reported that the homelands would not be able to survive and were not viable for independence.

Despite this, the government pushed ahead with its plans. Only four homelands were willing to co-operate namely, Transkei, Bophuthatswana, Venda and Ciskei.

Leaders of the other six Bantustans refused and argued that it would be economic suicide to go it alone. The idea of losing South African citizenship was also a major deterrent. The creation and acceptance of Bantustan meant the government could now force people to live there.

Under Article 1 (12) of the Charter of the United Nations, one of the purposes of the United Nations is to develop friendly relations among nations based on respect for the principle of equal rights and self-determination of people...The conditions for the exercise of the right are

• That there exists a people within the meaning of the article
• That a determination of their political status is made by that people
• That this determination is made freely
• That the people are free to pursue their economic, social and cultural development.

The government, however, formulated the proposals and decided which people and what territories they applied to. Any attempt to oppose the policy was ruthlessly repressed under laws supposedly formulated to protect the national security. Furthermore, the government claiming to create these independent states under the principle of self determination, is one which itself cannot claim legitimacy since it violates the principle of equal rights by denying all political rights to over 80% of the population on the basis of racial discrimination. It represented only the dominant white racial minority and not "the whole people belonging to the territory. Therefore, the supposed granting of independence to Bantustans could be compared with a gift by a thief of stolen property.

The whole Bantustan programme, like the original "native reserves", had been devised and formulated by the whites to maintain economic subjection of the African and ensure the continuance of a plentiful labour force in the white areas, where Africans had no political rights. The territories of the Bantustans were not coherent pieces of land; their frontiers were drawn in such a way as to exclude the lands of powerful white settlers or white-owned industries.

The territories of Bophuthatswana and Ciskei each with a little over half-a-million inhabitants, but with many hundreds of thousands living outside their boarders, were divided into 19 separate areas, not counting so-called "black spots". Of the four supposedly independent states, the smallest, Venda, had in 1970, 67% of its allotted population living in the territory concerned. Ciskei and Transkei had 55% and Bophuthatswana only 36%.

The purpose of this policy was to convert all Africans working in white areas into aliens, with no right to remain in the territory when they were no longer required as part of the labour force. As a South African minister of the interior stated: "We are looking forward to a situation in the near future where there will not be a single black citizen within the so-called white South Africa." This led to heartless mass population transfers through deportations involved in resettlement programmes.

Bophuthatswana was internationally known as the home of that great casino resort complex, Sun City. Big American performers and athletes earned rich rewards for appearances at the pleasure centre, which catered mainly for white South Africans. Leisure pursuits, forbidden elsewhere in Calvinist South Africa, flourished in Sun City. Yet behind this luxurious façade, the people of Bophuthatswana lived in terrible poverty, while the Bantustan itself played a central role in South Africa's apartheid system.

Bophuthatswana consisted of seven main pieces of land, located in three different provinces of South Africa. The 1980 resident population was estimated at two million people with an annual growth rate of over four percent.

The South African government claimed that each Bantustan was the real homeland for a particular ethnic group. The Batswana in the case of Bophuthatswana were stripped of South African citizenship and arbitrarily made citizens of the new "country", even if they had never lived in or visited the Bantustan.

The white minority government justified the complete denial of political rights for Africans in South Africa on the grounds that Africans would exercise these rights in the Bantustans. The vast majority of the Tswana rejected this system.

The government of Bophuthatswana consisted of a National Assembly of 72 elected members, and 24 members nominated by local chiefs. In the first elections for the National Assembly in 1977, only 163 141 people, or 12% of those eligible in Bophuthatswana cast their votes. Polling booths were set up in urban areas outside the Bantustans for Tswana residents to vote. At this time some 300 000 Tswana people lived in Soweto. Only 600 voted in the 1977 elections. In 1982, only 135 voted.

Since 1976 Chief Lucas Mangope headed the government as President. The vast majority of the people of Bophuthatswana were poor, but Mangope was not. In an area where the per capita income was estimated at between US$339 and US$495 US, Chief Mangope it is alleged, received a salary of US$27 500 a year and ran an expense account.

Bophuthatswana was marketed as a showcase Bantustan and proudly boasted a Bill of Rights. On paper it guaranteed equality before the law, the right to freedom from degrading punishment, and the right to freedom and liberty. But in reality, the opposition was seriously curtailed. The government maintained the power of detention without trial, and the right to declare any organisation illegal. Chiefs had considerable power and could arrest and pass sentence for certain offences.

Independence did not change the basic economic function of Bophuthatswana as a labour reservoir for white-owned mines, farms and industry. In 1982, over 12% of migrant workers from Bophuthatswana worked in the white areas. Another 163 000 people living in Bophuthatswana "commuted" to work in white areas because they were not allowed to live in those areas.

Bophuthatswana had taken a hostile attitude towards black trade unions emerging in South Africa. The Minister of Manpower was Rowan Cronje, a former Rhodesian labour minister in the white minority government of Ian Smith. A new labour law based on the Rhodesian model took effect in 1984. Under this legislation, unions based outside the Bantustan were barred from operating.

Instead of building houses for ordinary people, the Bophuthatswana government was spending US$120 million dollars on a capital, Mmabatho. Four hundred new houses were included in the plans, but were selling at a minimum of US$1 300 012 and were beyond reach for all but a tiny percentage of the people.

During the 1976 uprisings that began in Soweto, students in Bophuthatswana boycotted classes and burned down schools, government buildings and vehicles. On August 9, students burned down the Legislative Assembly building to dramatise their rejection of Bantustan independence. President Mangope's son was one of the students arrested during the uprisings.

Fearing the challenge to his rule, Mangope openly sided with the white minority government. He told a group of parents that the police had been lenient when dealing with strikes. "They should shoot indiscriminately. In fact, I have told the police to shoot even my own child," Mangope said.

Sun City was a US$90million dollar pleasure resort inserted into the vast rural poverty of Bophuthatswana. It played a significant part in the South African effort to break out of its isolation and win back foreign favour. The large complex included an artificial lake, a casino, soft porn movies, discotheques, and troops of scantily clad chorus girls. Nearby, the Pilansberg Game Reserve was created for the tourists' delight by evicting 100 families from their homes.

Audiences were not officially segregated at Sun City. But the cost of the more expensive tickets usually made this the *de facto* reality. Liza Minelli performed her opening night to a crowd of 4 500 people of which about 200 were blacks. There was only one black face in the most expensive seats. The rest were high up in the auditorium in seats that sold for $13 000. In addition, the Southern Sun, which owns the hotel, admitted to giving free tickets to blacks. It did so, not out of generosity but so that the artists did not perform to all-white audiences. "I don't mind about anything except that I'm playing in front of mixed audiences," Liza is alleged to have exclaimed, naively unaware that by performing there at all she was helping apartheid score a major propaganda coup.

Sun City, sometimes referred to as Sin City, existed as it did largely because of the apartheid fiction of independence. Laws in South Africa, which were *illegal,* like gambling, or sex between mixed races, did not apply in Bophuthatswana. It was unusual for black men to come to Bophuthatswana to do what they could not do in Johannesburg.

This led to the growth of prostitution. White men could go home to Johannesburg while black women had to stay in the poverty of the Bantustan. To suggest that casual integrated sex and black access to slot machines would break down the structures of apartheid was an insult to the long and costly struggle blacks had waged against oppression of minority rule. Because Sun City helped camouflage the reality of that rule, it did far more damage than good to the people of Bophuthatswana.

The fact was that political and economic interests were part and parcel of apartheid-controlled Sun City. The Bophuthatswana government, which would not have existed if it were not for apartheid, held a minority interest in the resort, as did a number of South African companies.

Not all performers had succumbed to the large sums offered to appear in Sun City. There was a growing list of those who refused lucrative contracts. As protests mounted against those who did go to Sun City performers, the ranks of those who put conscience before cash also grew.

In its submission to the 1997 Truth and Reconciliation Commission (TRC) hearings into business and apartheid, the Congress of South African Trade Unions (COSATU) explained:

*Capitalism in South Africa was built and sustained precisely on the basis of the systematic racial oppression of the majority of our people...Employers collaborated with the apartheid regime from the outset, supported apartheid in all its manifestations and benefited from apartheid capitalism with its exploitative and oppressive nature.*

*Maggie as a primary school teacher at Bethel primary school. She is training a group of sunbeams.*

# The Struggle In Phokeng

◆

In 1951, the Nationalist Government in one of its endeavours to exclude Blacks from parliament and from urban areas, abolished the Native Representative Council. Black reserves were grouped into ten territories and each would become a homeland for a potential African "nation". Each territory would be administered by a "Bantu authority", under white supervision. These authorities consisted mainly of hereditary chiefs. Every such "nation" would be allowed to develop along its own lines with homeland residents enjoying all the rights they were denied in the Republic of South Africa.

This piece of legislation, Verwoerd's brainchild, was completed in 1971. The Bantu Homeland Constitution Act empowered Pretoria to grant independence to any homeland.

In 1976, the Transkei - the present Eastern Cape - was the first homeland to come into being. The first president was Kaizer Matanzima. Bophuthatswana followed in 1977, with Lucas Mangope as its first and only president. Next was Venda in 1979, headed by Mphephu, and finally Ciskei in 1981 with Oupa Qoso as president.

Homeland "independence" deprived citizens of their rights of South African citizenship. In Bophuthatswana, as in all "independent" homelands, we were forced to discard our South African identity documents. In their place we were issued a new document called Ikitse "Know Yourself". We surrendered our South African passports for Lokwalo lwa Mosepele - "Letter of Travel" - which was recognized only in the neighbouring states of Botswana, Lesotho and Swaziland. The new document was not accepted in the international community. It therefore posed a problem for Bophuthatswana citizens wanting to visit, or study in other countries abroad.

I used my South African passbook for a long time after independence. Even my documents with the Education Department reflected my South African identity number.

Around 1986 or 1987, while I was lecturing at Tlhabane College, a circular from the Department of Education instructed all those without Bophuthatswana identity documents to obtain them immediately or their salaries would be withheld. The salaries, we learned, were already in the rector's office. We had no alternative but to rush to the local Home Affairs office to make applications. We were instructed to surrender our South African documents after applying.

I refused to surrender mine. The excuse I gave was that I had lost it. I retained it secretly because I knew I would need it some day. It was a dangerous decision though, but I was prepared to live with the risk.

I used this South African document to make an application for an international passport in Pretoria. No problem! For a residential address I used St. Joseph's Catholic Mission, which though situated on a patch of South African land, served the people of Phokeng who were legally deemed - or doomed - to live in Bophuthatswana.

In my possession I held several government documents from Bophuthatswana and South Africa.

Bophuthatswana, like most other homelands, consisted of several pieces of land, separated by white-owned farms, and sometimes by towns and dorpies. In Bophuthatswana there were 19 fragments, some hundreds of miles apart. Governments of homelands were dependent on subsidies from Pretoria.

The oppression experienced in these homelands was even worse than that of South Africa. The possible cause of this was closely-knit structures which constituted the social fabric. Community members all knew each other so it was easy for the president of Bophuthatswana to know what each aspiring local leader was up to.

Because of sheer poverty and hunger many people became informants for the homeland government and were rewarded with promotion to higher positions and some nice perks. The homeland regime had little difficulty in creating vacancies for such informants.

There were many employed officials who had virtually nothing to do in their offices. You might come across them quietly reading children's literature at their desks or playing cards during an extended lunch break. In public they were highly visible in the entourage of the president when he visited remote communities in the homeland.

President Lucas Mangope controlled every nook and cranny of Bophuthatswana. He would go personally to close a university when students were rioting, he dictated verdicts at court, had the capacity to fire an official of any department by telephone at home at night and dictated who should be friends with whom. If by any chance you happened to be in his bad books he would isolate you. You would be surprised to find that some people avoided you in public for fear of a tongue-lashing from the boss. He also found it convenient to summon a citizen from hundreds of miles away just to deliver a reprimand.

If you befriended someone who was isolated by Mangope, you ran the danger of losing your job. He used people like they were his pawns. Yet he never ceased to tell audiences about "the God that he loved and trusted and served...the God that loved him". Sometimes it was scary listening to his speeches. Fundamentally, his policies and prayers did not match. I would immediately switch off my TV rather than listen to what sounded to me like so much hypocrisy.

Under the homeland regime, common criminals could be set free depending on their political connections. On the other hand, innocent people were imprisoned and humiliated, especially if they posed a challenge to the president or any of his inner circle.

Many authors and media houses exposed oppression of blacks in urban areas, but very little has been documented about rural areas in general, and rural homeland communities in particular. It was for this reason that those who supported activists in South Africa ignored those who were suffering in the homelands. Yet the people who found themselves trapped in homelands formed the majority of blacks in rural South Africa. Homeland citizens became orphans in the land of their forefathers. Lacking international recognition, homelands were destined to remain in a political limbo where citizens went largely unnoticed.

Many people were opposed to the homeland or Bantustan system, but dared not express their views. Criticism of the system landed many in prison or cost them their jobs or both. Yet many agreed that Bantustans were but a political sham; a temporary arrangement based largely on Pretoria's divide-and-rule strategy which would inevitably collapse some day.

Were we blacks ever consulted when the homelands system was being planned? The system was but a deal between the authorities in Pretoria and their compliant homeland chiefs. Many considered these leaders to be mere puppets. Imagine the fury when it dawned on us blacks that we had been robbed of our rights. No longer South African citizens, just who were we? The outside world did not recognise us.

We would have to work very hard to alert the international community to our suffering. In 1990, the Women Ministries of the South African Council of Churches delegated me to visit Switzerland at the invitation of the Swiss Federation of Christian Women. My task was to alert the Swiss to the suffering of women in South Africa, giving special emphasis to the homeland. Many were to hear of the homelands - and of suffering homelands - for the very first time! Others did not comprehend what I was talking about. However, they were eager to learn.

I attended many conferences convened by the South African Council of Churches, SACC, and the Institute of Contextual Theology, where we discussed in depth the sufferings of the oppressed homeland citizens, whose cries were not being heard by the outside world. I think we succeeded in exposing Bophuthatswana's poor civil rights record and in putting our people on par with the rest of South Africa's oppressed masses.

We also fought hard for our detainees in the homeland. They would have to be granted the status of political prisoners. The Mangope regime aimed at presenting them as common criminals and was determined to hide their existence.

From 1988 matters began to improve. The SACC insisted on placing the status of men and women in the homeland prisons on the agenda of international conferences. You can imagine the hopes that were raised in Rooigrond Maximum Prison in the then Mmabatho!

Indeed homelands were designed to perpetuate oppression of black people by their puppet black leaders. "Lords of poverty", these leaders became filthy rich while their own people became poorer and poorer. Pretoria paid them well to do their dirty job, and they conformed. Children and relatives of President Mangope lived in luxury and opulence. They held the best jobs and owned a number of businesses and properties. The homeland might have collapsed but these people are still wealthy today.

The apartheid regime took land away from communities with the assistance and approval of homeland leaders. Many political activists arrested in Bophuthatswana were deported to South Africa to be tortured and tried there. This happened because homeland police were not yet as experienced in dealing with such offenders as their white counterparts in South Africa.

When you became a teacher in Bophuthatswana you were automatically enrolled as a member of the Bophuthatswana Teachers' Association (BTA). Your membership fee was deducted from your monthly salary. As a result of this coercion many of us boycotted the meetings of this body. Elections of BTA office bearers were a sham and disguise as the government had secretly determined the membership of the executive.

There was also a body of ministers of religion called the Bophuthatswana Ministers Fraternal (Bomifra). This body worked hand-in-glove with the regime to implement the wishes of their president. However, not all church leaders were aligned to this body. Probably the majority of Baruti strove to keep well clear of party politics altogether. At the other end of the spectrum, there were those prophetic voices that followed what the Gospel taught them. They became the voice of the voiceless. Inevitably, this latter group of clerics frequently found themselves in trouble with the Bophuthatswana regime.

One such person was the Bishop of the Catholic Diocese of Rustenburg, Kevin Dowling. He was never scared to confront President Mangope about the suffering of the citizens of Bophuthatswana, in particular that of Phokeng. When people could not face Mangope, Bishop Kevin Dowling became their spokesperson. He vigorously defended the queen-mother of the Bafokeng, Mrs Semane Molotlegi, against unlawful arrest. At the height of the struggle, he defended people's basic right of association, allowing them free access to the premises of St Joseph's. But he is just one example.

It was a time of painful transition and some churches stepped forward and gave the lead through their style of witness. To them, liberation would embrace both the political and the religious aspects. Clerics known to me, who took a public stand for Gospel values were the Rev. Molete, secretary of the Rustenburg Council of Churches, Rev. Tselapedi and Rev Tawana.

In the Rustenburg-Phokeng area pastors such as these grouped themselves and held weekly prayer meetings in response to the political upheavals all around them. The venue for these prayer meetings rotated from one church premise to another. Thus if Rev George Dalke hosted the interdenominational prayer meeting one evening in his Tlhabane Lutheran Church, next week the venue might be St. Peter's, and the leader, Fr Dan Rishton, or Fr Sean Lunney; or the group would be warmly welcomed to St Joseph's by Fr Gerry McCabe, a fearless critic of the homeland.

The agenda at such meetings embraced much more than prayer, however. Topics such as the biblical origins of human rights, basic freedoms, and many aspects of democratic governance were frequently raised. Pastors were also kept updated on the fate of local detainees whose intentions would then be prayed for. The De La Salle community at St Joseph's kept itself well abreast of the transition. Br Joseph, Br Finbarr, Sr Georgina and Sr Monica Duffy opened their doors wide to all in need, and embraced the new South Africa through their creative work in education, health services, and media such as West newspaper. All these men and women of the cloth representing their various churches were outspoken in their defence of the voiceless.

Because the regime banned all meetings of the Bafokeng people and all political parties in the struggle, St. Joseph's Catholic Church, which is the seat of Bishop Kevin Dowling, became a popular meeting place.

When Rocky Malebana-Metsing staged his dramatic return to Bophuthatswana in November 1992, he selected the grounds of St Joseph's Mission in Phokeng for a major welcoming rally. Rocky, by now transformed into an ANC stalwart, could not have chosen a more strategic venue. St Joseph's occupies a patch of ground which was surrounded by but is independent from - three adjacent powers, South Africa, Bophuthatswana, and the Bafokeng. I sometimes reflect on the critical role played by St Joseph's Church in the struggle. It was the one and only safe refuge where people could turn to. From February 1988, the date of the aborted coup, to the collapse of Bophuthatswana in early 1994, St Joseph's was the only venue unconditionally available to the public for political meetings and rallies.

All those parties and alliances banned in Bophuthatswana enjoyed free access to the church premises. These banned organizations included the Bafokeng, the ANC, COSATU, the Pan-African Congress, AZAPO, the Communist Party, the Women's League, as well as the youth structures attached to these groups. As the tensions heightened following the release of Nelson Mandela in February 1990, the banned organizations had to depend solely on St Joseph's. In fact the weekends were so busy with meetings and the demand for space so pressing that schedules had to be established for Saturday mornings, for Saturday afternoons, and for Sunday afternoons. Sunday mornings were reserved for Mass.

Although South Africa had lifted the ban on all political organisations well before Mandela's release, Bophuthatswana had chosen a different course. These organizations were viewed as a direct threat to the homeland, and therefore their official activities, conferences, meetings or rallies would be tolerated nowhere within the borders of Bophuthatswana.

Where else could banned groups turn to, if not the churches? And St Joseph's was available and convenient. Thousands of Bophuhatswana citizens of all political persuasions resided within comfortable walking and talking - distance of these grounds, where the gate was always open, and fences were totally porous.

Furthermore, the new bishop living at St Joseph's, Bishop Kevin Dowling, was known to emphasise Catholic social teachings. It followed therefore that issues of justice and peace, and human rights generally, stood high among his priorities. He had held resolute in defence of the rights of political and civil organizations to use his church premises, despite a serious warning by way of a bomb explosion in the sanctuary, when Fr Eddie Corish was parish priest. This ugly incident took place soon after Nelson Mandela's release in 1990. Now over two years later, the battle lines were more clearly demarcated and the political tensions were rising by the day. Bophuthatswana was feeling nervous and its rhetoric was becoming more defiant. At all costs, those meetings at St Joseph's had to be stopped!

You must consider yet another source of tension. To the west and north, the church grounds formed a common boundary with South Africa. In fact the church site once formed part of Paul Kruger's own original farm. This land at the time we are discussing was occupied by Afrikaner farmers; many more Afrikaners found skilled employment in the local mines. The political outlook of this minority tended, at best, to be conservative. After all, how could they reasonably be expected to join ranks with the newly unbanned ANC? But there was yet a more worrying factor: Eugene Terreblanche that bellicose protagonist of white supremacy lived in Ventersdorp, just an hour's drive away.

This Afrikaner presence added to the mounting tensions within Bophuthatswana in general and Phokeng in particular. They were on our doorstep.

Rocky's come-back rally in November was widely publicised in the media which speculated frantically on how he might cope with Bophuthatswana's road blocks or whether on the other hand, he would be accorded some measure of diplomatic immunity. Both lines of thought missed the mark. Rocky chose to land by helicopter! His very first task was to thank the bishop for allowing the rally to go ahead, despite last night's disaster.

About 5 000 turned out for this political meeting, a meeting that Bophuthatswana could not control. It passed without incident - and this despite the usual heavy military display. At all major rallies at St Joseph's, South African Casspirs, police armoured vehicles, parked themselves on the Boshoek side of the entrance, while Bophuthatswana's vehicles occupied the Phokeng side.

On the Monday prior to the rally Bishop Dowling was visited by a high-powered delegation from Mafikeng. Their request was simple, yet grave: Refuse the use of the St Joseph's church grounds for the forth-coming rally because such meetings were destabilising Bophuthatswana. This was the president's urgent request; and anyway didn't the bishop know from his previous encounter with the president and cabinet just how serious a threat those ongoing mass meetings at St Joseph's were posing. The delegates persisted with their requests and veiled threats for a full three hours, ignoring the fact that the bishop had only just returned from hospital where he had undergone serious surgery.

His response? Since political activity was so restricted in Bophuthatswana, and all but the main political party banned, where were activists to turn to? Basically, he had to instruct his reluctant visitors on the core democratic freedoms: Freedom of speech, of religious belief, of expression, of association. How could he as a church leader conspire to deny ordinary citizens their God-given human rights - especially at a time of major transition? No, he as bishop could never refuse the church grounds for the coming Saturday rally.

And that was the message the reluctant delegates were to take to the authorities in Mafikeng; but the authorities in Mafikeng sent back their own devastating message.

On Friday morning at two o'clock sharp, residents of St Joseph's Mission awoke to a deafening blast. The church, new building though it was, had been bombed. The job was done by implosion, rather that explosion, and seemed executed by remote control. The sight that confronted Fr Vincent Brennan, parish priest, was ghastly: smashed statues, broken furniture, collapsed ceilings and splintered rafters. Fragments of coloured glass were scattered widely around outside. The figure of the Crucified with broken hands and feet, lay face-down on the floor. It was a horrible sight, a symbol of ultimate desolation. Yet to this day, no culprit has been apprehended for this sacrilege.

Rocky and his comrades had every reason to thank the bishop. Bophuthatswana had done its best to block that Saturday rally, and had failed. The meeting had gone ahead, providing the ANC cohorts with a double victory. For Bophuthatswana it was a double disaster.

We didn't use the Catholic Church for meetings and rallies only; it was also a secret refuge. I myself spent days hiding there for fear of being arrested. Mrs. Semane Molotlegi, queen-mother and spouse of Kgosi Lebone, also found refuge at St. Joseph's whenever she visited Phokeng, as she was banned from Bophuthatswana and from visiting her Legato residence. We occupied separate rooms at the De La Salle community. Some Bafokeng leaders would sneak in to meet their queen in secret.

These activities in Phokeng were being monitored in Mafikeng daily. If President Mangope feared St Joseph's as the rock where his ship of state would founder, he was getting the big picture right. In the final confrontation in which Bishop Dowling was summoned before the Bop cabinet, he was warned that since St Joseph's Mission continued to destabilise the homeland, then Bophuthatswana could take whatever steps were necessary to defend itself.

At a Mass in Holy Week in 1993, the bishop, clearly under stress, explained the acute security risk the missionaries at St Joseph' were now facing. If the regime had bombed the church twice already, what would the newest threat unleash? Therefore the physical safety of the missionaries could not be guaranteed a day longer; they were free to quit the premises in the interests of their personal safety, and go elsewhere. They stayed put.

I sometimes dream of a great reconciliation service being organised at St Joseph's in Phokeng where we could all once more embrace each other and embrace our common future. In terms of our struggle for North-West, has St Joseph's not played a role similar to that of Regina Mundi in Soweto? Has the time not come to recognize this fact?

**Above** - *Maggie as District Manager of Education-Rustenburg.*

**Left** - *Maggie as District Manager.*

# Facing The Mountain

◆

The politics in Bophuthatswana were changing rapidly during my years at
Tlhabane College of Education. The official opposition party had always
been Seopasengwe; its leader was Mr. Victor Sefora. But during this period a
second party emerged and seemed to mature quickly. This party was known as
the Peoples Progressive Party (PPP), and it was led - or misled - by Rocky
Malebana Metsing. Members of this party lived or worked mostly in and around
Rustenburg and Phokeng.

At the time of the birth of this party, the president of Bophuthatswana was
waging war against the king and his Bafokeng tribe accusing them of disloyalty.
It is therefore little wonder that the PPP would be associated with the king and
his family and that it drew most of its members from the Phokeng area.

But things reached a climax in February 1988 when the PPP leader and some
members of the army staged a coup. Listening to radio news one morning we
were appalled to learn that the PPP leader had overthrown the government of the
homeland and handed it over to the army.

My husband had been an executive member of the party and at none of their
meetings had they discussed a coup. Later, when some of us were already in
prison, we were told exactly how the coup started and what transpired. We were
shocked.

The PPP, like all political parties, had an executive structure in place. Before
anything crucial is undertaken, it is obvious the executive would have dealt with
it in a meeting, and adopted a suitable plan of action. But it seems that the leader
of the party was so ambitious that he plotted the coup in collusion with only a

few members of the army. It later transpired that they had already positioned themselves in the cabinet should the coup succeed. Mr. Malebane-Metsing was to be the president. Many people agreed at the time that should he have succeeded, he would have been no better than the then president of the homeland. In fact, he would have been more of a despot than the one we knew.

News later emerged that on the very night preceding the coup there were PPP members in his house but did not know what was going on. We heard reports of visitors coming and going the whole night through. All were surprised the next morning when the South African Army surrounded the house and they were arrested. In the meantime, Rocky had already escaped into exile claiming to have fought for the rights of the people of the homeland. But the question arises as to what his real agenda was.

As the news of the coup broke, the president and his ministers were being held hostage at the Mmabatho Stadium, while Rocky had already donned the presidential attire. He was ready to occupy the presidential residence. But the whole plot went hopelessly wrong when the coup leaders phoned Pretoria reporting their achievements and stating their immediate plans. There was no way Pretoria would have created homelands and then allowed opportunists to destroy them like that.

In no time the South African Army had surrounded the stadium and freed the hostages. Many coup leaders were arrested. Rocky and PPP member Lamola managed to flee the country. They had been cute enough to prepare their exit in advance, should the coup abort. Plan B worked.

Not only were those around the stadium arrested but all over the homeland, people belonging to the PPP - active member or not - and those suspected of being anti-government were all apprehended. President Mangope cast his net wide.

I too would be netted - and sooner than I thought. I was in class as usual with my Primary Diploma students on the morning of 15th February, two days after the aborted coup, when I was urgently summoned to the rector's office. Two police officers informed me verbally that I was to appear immediately before Captain Hlakanye. The rector, Miss Beauty Malefo, posed two questions before we left her office: would Mrs. Bopalamo return, and what official entry should she make in the staff logbook regarding Mrs Bopalamo's immediate absence.

I remember my feelings being driven out of Tlhabane College of Education.

I was puzzled by this nonsense I was being dragged into. I who was not a member of PPP or any other party, I who had never attended a political rally of any sort, I who was attending to my professional duties up to this very hour: how come I was now being hauled off to a police station? What crime had I committed? I felt indignation and anger too at this unprovoked and vulgar police action. And there was the sense of betrayal: why hadn't the rector defended me?

After all, she - and not any police officer - was my immediate superior in our line of command. I felt thrown to the wolves. But was I afraid? No, never! Why should I be? My conscience was clear.

Arriving at the Phokeng Police Station, I realized I was not alone. There were familiar faces of detainees, my husband Solly among them, awaiting Hlakanye's next order. I had wanted to question this Hlakanye guy, to interrogate him even, about my civil liberties, my basic human rights. I demanded an explanation. But no, no! He could say nothing; I'd get answers to all my queries when I got to Mafikeng. This Hlakanye was later reputed to be one of the most notorious officers in the whole of Bophuthatswana. He liked to strike at the dead of night.

We were transported in the back of the police van where I was the only female. It was raining. I acutely needed to visit a bathroom on the way to Mafikeng but the officers driving us would not agree to stop. The men in the van, including my husband, also pleaded with these policemen, but they remained adamant.

Late at night we arrived at Mafikeng Police Station. I was escorted to an all-women cell. I had never experienced such filth before. Everything was so filthy and stinking that I could not even think of wrapping myself in a blanket. We all lay on the floor with blankets spread. The floor was uncomfortably wet and the stench coming from the toilet was unbearable.

The women I found in the cell had been arrested for various offences. Some of them were drunk. There was a Sangoma, a person who communicates with the ancestors, who made terrifying screams the whole night, communicating with them. Prisoners seemed to ignore her completely and it was left to a charitable colleague to calm her down.

It was a coincidence that after hours of mental and spiritual torture, I discovered someone who was as terrified as me. She was a schoolteacher from

Taung. She too had been nabbed at school. Flora's school flask and sandwiches, still untouched, would provide our supper. The two of us stayed awake the whole night.

In the morning Flora and I, together with the men who were in our company the previous day, were summoned. We had not reached our destination yet. Driving through town, the police officer stopped in Mafikeng. This officer realised that we had neither supper the previous night, nor breakfast that morning. We were allowed to buy food before being taken to Rooigrond Maximum Prison, where we would be detained for the next fourteen days.

The cell in which we were held was very big. There were about a 100 women from all parts of Bophuthatswana - so-called "Enemies of the State". Sprawled on blankets on both sides of the cell, we became a united force. Wardresses had little choice but to befriend us. The atmosphere here was different from that of Mafikeng Police Station. The cell was neat. We also found time for toiletry. The Queen of the Bafokeng Mrs Semane Molotlegi was among us. Our loyalty to her did not end because of incarceration; we did not lose ourselves. We sang, prayed, joked, and discussed new strategies. Indeed, like the Rivonia prisoners on Robben Island, prison became our university. We would emerge as graduates in political science, majoring in the praxis of course, but without the bit of paper.

All the women were interrogated. One old woman from Ga-Rankuwa when asked what she knew about overthrowing the government (menolo puso) said. "My hands are so weak and feeble, how on earth could I topple something as huge as a government?" After 14 days of interrogation, we women were released, except for Mrs. Malebana-Metsing, The authorities hoped she would divulge her husband's whereabouts. How wrong they were. She knew nothing.

The men, including my husband, Solly, were not released. Kgosi Lebone of the Bafokeng was among them. After his release, he escaped mysteriously to Botswana and returned only in 1994. After re-settling in Phokeng he remained sickly, never fully recovering from the ordeal of imprisonment. He died shortly thereafter.

It was as if detention had ignited my activism. I ran around to secure legal representation for those in prison. They had already been charged with treason, and refused bail. I kept Priscilla Jana, the attorney in Johannesburg, fully informed. She also sent information through me. One young man, Musi

Bogopane, who died in a mysterious car crash, supported me every way until his death.

Soon the Special Branch got to know about our movements. I was taken from work constantly to be interrogated at the Bafokeng Civic Centre where they rented offices.

The St. Joseph's Mission became the hub of our activities. Clandestine meetings with lawyers were convened. The Catholic Bishop of Rustenburg, Bishop Kevin Dowling, the De La Salle Brothers Joseph and Finbarr, and also Sister Georgina, all proved very helpful. They opened their doors for such meetings to take place. The shocking thing was that some of our people could not keep any secrets. I had to answer what the meetings at St. Joseph's Mission were all about every time they were held. But that was not going to stop us. Some of the people were too old to be stopped from speaking.

On the other hand, Phokeng was clearly divided into those supporting the royal family, and those supporting Mangope. Whenever these two groups met, there was a war of words. Secret meetings which had been convened, were divulged when one group boasted to the other about the achievement reached with lawyers

Some time in April or May of 1988, another lady - whose husband was in prison and I were called by the PPP leader who was then in Harare to fetch money for payment of lawyers who represented our men. We drove in my bakkie, a charcoal-coloured Volkswagen, to Botswana. We were referred to a lady at the Botswana travel agency. We were joined there by one of the PPP members. The man had technically escaped arrest as he was in the executive of the party. The rest of the executive was in prison.

I possessed a valid passport of the Republic of South Africa. It was not unusual for a person of Bophuthatswana to posses this type of passport if you played the right cards. When I applied for the identity document of the Republic of South Africa, I said my address was St. Joseph's Catholic Church. St Joseph's Mission was in the Republic of South Africa but its land abutted Bophuthatswana to the east. The officials at the Department asked what I did there at the Mission, and I told them I was a teacher there.

One of the officials at Home Affairs probably knew me. He was a young man- same age group as my sons. It is possible for young people to know you very well while you can barely recognise them. The young man had quite a sense of humour. He asked an interesting question, which makes me laugh even today : "So Mama, how are Kennedy, Magae and Harold doing?" These are my children. It was just a joke. He was going to fix my documents anyway.

Saint Joseph's Mission serves the people of Phokeng and is situated on a portion of the farm once belonging to Paul Kruger. The site was purchased by the church and it was situated and was bordered by the territories of Bophuthatswana; namely Phokeng; and the Republic of South Africa; namely, the municipality of Boshoek.

However, I did not throw away my Ikitse; the Bophuthatswana identity document. I also went further to apply for a Lokwalo lwa mosepele, a passport of the homeland, which could only take me as far as neighbouring states like Botswana or Lesotho.

My two companions did not have valid documents to enter Zimbabwe. However arrangements were made before hand to allow them to cross using these ambiguous papers they were given in Botswana. At Harare airport we waited a long time to pass through customs.

Only after a tall gentleman, whom we did not know, intervened, were my colleagues allowed to go through. I had no problem. But they were to leave their documents behind and fetch them on departure. The custom officials clearly stated that they did not deal with Bantustan documents.

Ten days after our arrival back in South Africa, we were raided by the Special Branch. First it was my prison companion, Fanny Dlamini who was picked up. My comrades would approach me, challenging: "Do you know Fanny has been arrested. Are you going to wait around to be nabbed?"

I pondered. I had my ailing mother and my grandchildren to look after. So I refused the comrades' offer. I abandoned myself completely and prepared myself for the consequences of my actions.

We had a very cold winter that year and on a Saturday I went to Rustenburg to do shopping. Among the things I brought was a heater. Instinctively I was preparing myself for the worst. At midnight the knock came at my door. There was one group at the back of the house and another in front with rifles. There were three vehicles in all. One private car, a van and a truck. They were a mixture of police and the army.

They ransacked the house in a way that makes me close my eyes in disbelief when I remember the event. They asked for the passport I used to go to Harare. I gave them the homeland passport, the Lokwalo lwa mosepele. They insisted they wanted the real one, which they got. They went to my bakkie, the one I used to cross the border. There was money in the car; some of it was for people who applied for ANC cards. The other part of that money I had withdrawn from the bank for the family's use. Yes, as instinct had already warned me, they grabbed it all.

My granddaughter, Keamogetswe, was two and half years old at the time I faced this unpleasant ordeal at the hands of the Bophuthatswana police. She got up and came to stand in the passage looking at them with shock at the drama-unfolding inside her granny's house. This toddler looking at them in disbelief and wonder must have embarrassed the police. Their senior, shouted to my daughter, to take the child away. In his words "we don't want to see children here". True, their act was barbarically unethical and immoral. The sight of it would have affected any child. They knew this but still their consciences could not stop them. The love of money, status, and material things!

My eldest grandson, Kealeboga was eight years old at the time. Whenever he saw the president of Bophuthatswana on television, he switched it off, saying "I know he is going to talk about my grandpa and I don't want to see him."

These were unhealthy attitudes children were forced to adopt in Bophuthatswana. In crèches, children as young as three, sang about the president accusing him of the terrible treatment meted out to their parents. Some of the staff members, loyal to the regime, would lock up these children in classrooms as punishment. Their parents would then be reported to the powers that be, where they would be tongue-lashed about being a bad example for their children. Bophuthatswana was now under a reign of terror.

I was first driven in a white Mazda and somewhere on the way Captain Hlakanye said they were not going to be in the same car with a terrorist. I was then transferred to the back of the truck. It was very cold. The truck tossed me to and fro all the way until we arrived at Mogwase Police Station where they interrogated me until 10am the following day. I was then thrown in a cell alone. It was very cold. There was no blanket or anything to sit or sleep on. The toilet was leaking, water was flowing all over. I stood and alternatively squatted. Lunch was served to the other prisoners. I could see through the burglar door. The door was left open. I was not given anything to eat. I called the prisoners who served the food and inquired why I was not served. They said they were told not to speak to me.

In the evening again the same thing was repeated. One prisoner, who really sympathised with me, told the policeman who had reported for duty that I was in the cell and had not had anything to eat the whole day.

In my experience of the struggle I discovered that not all policemen and government officials were dishonourable. Some of them were good men and women. The policeman who came to my cell was very disgusted at how his colleagues had treated me. He took me out and offered me his share of supper. I wish I knew his name. After I had the first meal, in 24 hours, he transferred me to another cell, where other women I knew were detained. They had enough to eat, because of visitors. They also had blankets. They massaged my feet with Vaseline and put blankets over me. I slept like a log.

The atmosphere in this cell revived my dampened spirit. We talked about the politics of our homeland and cherished hopes for the future. But before breakfast was served the following morning, they came.

There was much squabbling and finger pointing about who had transferred "that woman" to another cell and how she was not supposed to mix with detainees of lesser offence. I was then hurled into a car. I did not know my destination. How could I? I did not care anymore.

We passed in front of my house in Phokeng and drove towards Mafikeng but after passing Zeerust, the car took a turn to Lehurutshe. At Zeerust, I requested to buy food with the money I was given by the women in the cell and I also visited the loo. We drove to Motswedi police station where in-depth interrogation would take place carried out by Special Branch officers from South Africa namely Loods, Gouws and Ackerman. It started as soon as we arrived. The first night I was alone in the cell.

My fellow detainees had revealed everything about our trip to Harare. I could sense this from the line of questioning taken and names of comrades we met.

"So tell us about Chris Hani and the new South Africa", they would taunt me. Chris Hani's name made them furious. Sometimes they ignored me and talked among themselves: "Bastard, they met him, Number so and so", mentioning the number of a person in exile from their album. They had an album of photos and next to the photo was attached a number, not the name of the person.

Our trip to Harare was a result of our discussions with the lawyers. They had advised us to raise funds as the trial and bail of the men in prison would cost a substantial amount of money. It was going to take a long time and funds would be exhausted before it came to completion.

Attorney Priscilla Jana had sought the services of very good advocates, Maizen and Kennedy. The latter was one of the legal people who visited us at our clandestine meetings at the De La Salle House at St. Joseph's Mission in Phokeng.

That night a woman who claimed to have been arrested for selling cosmetics without a licence, came to my cell. She told me it was actually her daughter who was selling and when they could not find her, she was taken into custody. We talked although I did not disclose much to her. What I said was that I was happy because when they arrested me, they did not take the phone book where the lawyers' phone numbers are kept; and that my daughter must have contacted them by then. This woman was actually a spy. She disclosed everything I had said.

Early the next day I was moved again. This time to Mafikeng Police Station, the filthiest place I ever experienced in my life. Again I requested the young policeman to get me food from town with the money I still had. The following morning I was taken to a building in town for interrogation. There I met my two colleagues who had accompanied me to Harare. I hadn't met them since my arrest. Different people interrogated us in separate rooms. From time to time our statements were checked and compared.

That night we were taken to Khupe. The Bophuthatswana Army used this as a prison. Those who transgressed regulations were held there. These were the same cells used for members of the army and they were very small. There was a bed, a toilet next to the bed, a chain fastened to an iron kept by cement on the floor. In other words those army members who were arrested received their meals by just stretching their arms while on the bed. The food was given through burglar doors. This was to be our home for the next fortnight.

We stayed here for a period of two weeks, being interrogated daily. One morning, at the end of the second week, it was so unusually quiet and we started to wonder what was to become of us. Word had spread that the commissioner of police complained that prisoners were treated like guests in a hotel. We were called out and hurled onto an open bakkie. We did not know where we were taken. Soon we were back at Mafikeng police station and would be there for one night.

On the following morning, a car came to fetch us. We had the opportunity on the way to converse with the police officer. He was alone. He was quite sympathetic. He said a number of them in Khupe thought we would be released but "the power above" would not agree to that. They wanted us to suffer more, just for opposing their government. We were heading for three months of detention - detention without trial.

*Maggie as parliament member at Nairobi (Kenya).*

# Guest Of The Government

◆

Arriving at Rooigrond prison, the main prison of the homeland, we were each given our individual cells.

My cell was just a few paces from the wardresses' office and the entrance. When my door was open, as happened most of the days, I could hear the conversations among wardresses and also see people coming in and out of the female prison. I could see those who were going to meet their visitors.

Next to me was a cell occupied by three women waiting to be hanged. Although I couldn't see them, I could sense their human misery. At one stage they would be singing beautiful hymns and praying. At another time they would be engaged in a furious fight. I felt pity for them. They were trapped in a state of complete depression, fear, frustration and confusion. One day a wardress had served food, and mistakenly left a knife on the tray. One of the inmates seized the knife and tried to commit suicide, but the others raised the alarm.

Up to this time my family did not know where to look for me. Relatives kept their ears to the ground. Some of the warders, who were once my students, though they had signed oaths of secrecy, felt no choice but to divulge my whereabouts to my family.

The one person who vowed he would know where I was, was my parish priest, Father Anthony Hunt. He did visit one day. As he came in through the entrance I could see him, and he saw me. As he talked to wardresses he was told that, I was not to be visited, nor was I to speak to anybody. But that didn't bother Fr Hunt. He came rushing in, dropping a piece of paper secretly which was a letter from my family. He hugged me and gave me the niceties that he had brought; biscuits, sweets and fruit. He hurriedly reported to me a lot of news before the women from the office intervened and hustled him out of my cell.

Some wardresses would allow me to go out for an hour while others preferred to keep me inside for the whole day.

Prison life is a terrible experience. At four in the afternoon you have your supper and you are then locked up until the next day. At six the next morning you have official prayer and only then the cells are unlocked. Sometimes, they would forget to unlock my door or even to pray with me. But Father Hunt had given me all the spiritual food I needed; the Bible, a prayer book, a meditation booklet and a hymn book. I did not rely on routine prison prayer.

Anyway, how much of it was truly sincere? It seemed to me to be far too much red tape. On Sundays my former students, warders from the male section, secretly threw newspapers into my cell. Wardresses who noticed this irregularity chose to ignore it.

One day officials of the prison came to search our cells because it was suspected that we had received written information from outside. One young wardress warned me, and as I cleaned the cell that morning, I made sure that only the religious books were left visible.

Then there were days when male inmates would be singing hymns in their cells. I have always said if you wanted to form a good choir go to prison! I have never listened to such beautiful singing. I also wondered whether after their release, they would continue to praise God as they did when incarcerated.

Female prisoners also sang and danced on Wednesdays during prayer meetings and at Sunday services. On Sundays, the singing and dancing continued in the courtyard until suppertime.

There were also children in prison, born there after mothers were sentenced. One particular child who was two years old when I was detained was very close to me because I always had sweets and biscuits secretly brought to me.

After three months in detention we were summoned to the regional court. Our charge was sedition. Sedition like treason is considered a very serious crime against the state.

I was Accused Number One. I was being charged with perpetrating the launch of a second coup. There was a letter, which I had brought from Harare and which I had published in the Sunday papers. The letter asked the government to release all political prisoners in the Bophuthatswana Homeland, failing which the February 1988 coup would look like a Sunday School picnic! Information had leaked that I was actually the person responsible for publishing the letter.

As awaiting-trial prisoners, we were now able to join as colleagues. My co-accused and I occupied the sick room of the female prison.

Before Christmas of 1988, I was taken seriously ill. I had to be hospitalised. In Bophelong Hospital I occupied a side ward alone. There was a woman, my husband's cousin, who worked in that ward. Because of her surname she was quickly switched to other wards when I arrived. The nursing staff was given instructions never to have any discussions with me. They were to administer treatment, and nothing else.

Policemen and women guarded me in shifts day and night. At the window of the ward outside there were police; at my door there were others, and still others at the gates. No-one was supposed to report my presence at the hospital. The fear was that I might be abducted from the hospital and escape.

One morning the doctor had to examine me and the policewoman wanted to come in. I informed her of my right to privacy, as a patient. She insisted, coerced by the man who was with her. But ill as I was, I fought back. Only then did the doctor come to my assistance by agreeing with what I said. All through my argument with the police woman this doctor remained suspiciously quiet. They took me to be stubborn because apparently they were poorly informed about the rights of patients.

My husband's cousin also had a cousin on her mother's side who was a nursing sister in my ward. She brought me secret messages and personal items. The police were not always alert. My son Kennedy was a doctor at Klerksdorp and he had friends among doctors and nurses in the hospital. All these people brought me messages. I just became an impossible patient for the police to guard.

One Sunday afternoon Kennedy arrived and the police woman on duty allowed him in, but begged him to be short; otherwise her job would be on the line. He brought me refreshments and other necessities.

Things got so tough for the police guarding me that the only alternative was to return me back to the cells even before I was well enough.

Christmas came and we celebrated it in prison with a lot of eats brought by family and friends. I had such an abundance that I would share with common prisoners and their children. Sometimes even the wardresses accepted offers from us prisoners.

I am glad that I contributed something positive while in prison awaiting trial. My educational achievements were well known. Wardresses who were studying Matric asked for my assistance, which I freely gave. I took their prescribed books and summarised portions for them. There were also inmates who could not read or write who asked for my assistance. Although we were not allowed by law to mix with them, in time they flocked to our cell when they could not be detected. Wardresses, despite all the rules and red tape, remain human beings. They chose to be flexible.

I loved Sundays when we sang and danced together and taught them some hymns.

The Catholic priest in Mafikeng, Father Shepherd, who has since passed away, would visit me on Wednesday mornings to bring me Holy Communion. My colleague became interested and asked to be converted to Catholicism. Father Shepherd also brought me messages from my priest in Phokeng and from families and friends. Soon the instructions reached prison authorities that Catholic priests should be barred from visiting prisoners. This did not come as a surprise.

The new Catholic priest who later came to visit was black. It became clear to us that he was commissioned to deliver the official political agenda. He tried to convince us in his sermon about loyalty to our government. He stopped coming quite soon after he was introduced to us. We did not show any interest in him. The rapport that existed between us and Father Shepherd did not exist with him.

Some time after my release from prison and acquittal by the court of law, I met this priest in Victory Park, Johannesburg. I made him very uncomfortable, I think. He remained very withdrawn after I reminded him of where we had previously encountered each other.

New Year 1989 came. Lawyers, like most professionals, go for a break between Christmas and New Year. For quite some time our lawyers had been quiet. The only positive thing that my legal representative did when I was discharged from hospital was to compel the prison authorities to supply me with a bed. So I no longer slept on the floor. The lawyers had tried bail application but it was refused. We also fought for my colleague to be given a bed.

An interesting thing about Bophuthatswana was that the president controlled everything: universities and technikons, the justice system, hiring and firing of principals and teachers. The president also controlled the judiciary. Bop lawyers found themselves in a predicament. If they did not join the ruling party, they were declared an enemy of the state.

Sometime in March 1989, we went to court for the bail application. We succeeded. The South African Council of Churches paid R5 000 for each of us. Our attorney was Priscilla Jana but the Advocate who had to represent us in court was Morris Baslian, a very capable man. Students of the University of Bophuthatswana and some legal eagles flocked to court when learning that Morris Baslian was going to defend us. Coming out of court, they always remarked how much they learned from that man. He reduced the state's case to shreds, especially with regard to me. He proved that I had been in possession of valid documents when I crossed the South African border to enter Botswana, and thence to Harare. My passport had been stamped at these borders, and was used by the state as a major exhibit. But Baslian used the same exhibits to turn the tables on the state's case. It was an interesting case indeed.

Our trial dragged on to December 1989. Part of the condition of our bail was house arrest. That meant remaining in the house from six o'clock in the morning to six in the evening, when we reported to the police. We were not to leave the magisterial area of Bafokeng without permission from the Attorney General who happened to be based over 200km from Phokeng. If granted permission to travel, we would have to report what time we returned. Rustenburg town itself, about 9km from my home, was also deemed out of bounds.

In the first weeks of house arrest I would phone and seek permission to leave the magisterial area of Bafokeng, but soon I got tired of this ritual. I attended meetings and workshops in Gauteng and elsewhere. But all along, there was this feeling that prison was awaiting me. I had no freedom, or peace of mind. I took life step-by-step each day. The police too would never leave me alone. Casspirs would be parked outside my house at night with lights straight into my lounge. I shunned the lounge.

Word went around that my house was under surveillance by police and that those visiting risked arrest. I therefore lost some family members and friends who relied too much on rumour and hearsay. Only very close and sympathetic ones, and of course the political diehards and activists, and those who were sickened by the temporary set-up called a homeland, would risk coming to my house. I still went to church and Fr. Hunt visited me regularly. Bishop Kevin Dowling of Rustenburg remained a powerful resource person and compassionate friend. The De La Salle Brothers at St Joseph's supported me, as did the office of the South African Council of Churches in Rustenburg.

The village of Phokeng was divided into two groups: Those who were loyal to the Bophuthatswana government and those who opted for the royal family. Households were torn apart. Some had a poor grasp of politics, not realising that political affiliation in a progressive society is seldom a family affair. It does not necessarily follow that wife or husband, or even children all share the same political platform.

In Phokeng, the kgosi and queen had been forced into exile by the Bophuthatswana regime. The Bafokeng had within their ranks cohorts of loyalists and royalists who were ready to defend the throne, while at the same time there were those who cared not at all if the kgosi and queen never returned.

I hope the Bafokeng have learned a lesson that will guide them in the future and that there will never be a repetition of this sad episode. The exile of the kgosi affected many aspects of life. Political division was obvious everywhere and raised its ugly head in church. I soon found out that you had to be careful what you said aloud to God during the bidding prayers at Mass! Father Hunt often intervened because the anti-Bop prayers were proving so divisive. He had to; but some members of the congregation would complain bitterly to him.

Those who got involved in the struggle can stand tall and appreciate their hard work. Their energy was well spent. Some paid an enormous price, losing all they had. Others were denied their youth. Many were dismissed from their jobs and thus forfeited the pension funds due to them. Children who were left behind when parents were incarcerated grew up denied their human right to parental guidance and love. They too missed out in the natural process of growing up. They had to be adults overnight.

When the struggle against apartheid was waged, lucrative positions and personal gain were not the driving motivation, though there were exceptions of course. People did not fight primarily for elections, but rather to free their people from oppression. Was not the whole struggle aimed at redeeming the future generations?

We should not lose sight of the fact that apartheid was a monster that had to be fought in different ways and on different fronts. There were those who were not publicly known as freedom fighters and yet who supported activists materially and financially. Others spent long days in prayer. Others again supported the families of those behind bars and ran the risk of visiting the detainees. The struggle produced armies of unsung heroes and heroines.

Today the gains of victory are obvious for all to see - and access. The doors of opportunity are wide open to those who wish to advance themselves. The political playing fields have been levelled and government is working overtime to restructure the economy and advance black empowerment. People are free to open any door and ask for help or advice, or even to complain.

There is freedom of movement. Those who can afford to live in suburbs are free to do so. There are inter-racial marriages. We enjoy freedom of expression and freedom of association

Some problems cannot be solved overnight. After all, apartheid had been reinforced more strictly year by year from 1948 onwards. Blacks trapped in their Bantustans received the same message repeated in a thousand different ways: they were incompetent and unfit for national leadership roles because by nature the Bantu were deemed inferior.

Ironically, 1948 was the year in which the United Nations General Assembly adopted the Universal Declaration on Human Rights. The purpose of this declaration was to promote and encourage respect for human rights and fundamental freedoms. The United Nations declaration expounds the personal, civil, political, economic, social, and cultural rights of all regardless of race, creed and colour that are limited only by recognition of the rights and freedoms of others, and of morality, public order, and the common good of all.

Therefore the greatest challenge facing us now is to redeem our own black self-esteem. If we truly believe that "black is beautiful" then how come we black women spend three times more than our white counterparts on cosmetics? Aluta continua, the struggle continues, but mainly in our minds. This psychological war within us has to be fought with all our might for our children's sake. It is an even tougher war than the former, but with love and understanding we are sure to gain victory.

# Dismissed, But A Secret Deal

◆

While at Khupe, Mafikeng, where we were held for questioning, I had a dream. My late father stood at the cell door and asked me how we would go to court while the others were absent. This was the second time in life that my father paid me a visit in a dream.

I was living and working at Hebron when he first appeared in my dreams. In my sleep I looked through the window facing the main gate. As it was in his lifetime, he was approaching very fast and very furiously. He did not enter the house. He stood outside, at the same window and inquired: "Where is your grandfather?" Grandfather in this case refers to uncle, my father's elder brother, ntatemogolo. Then he left. The weather that night, with storms and thunder, was as wild and furious as he was. When I woke up the next day, I had a bath and went home to visit Ntatemogolo and his family. His wife had suffered a stroke the previous day while weeding the garden.

But this time at Khupe, he was very gentle and sympathetic as if he felt the pain I was feeling.

One morning in December 1989, on the eve of our last court appearance, I went to check my detainee companion at home. She was not there and her neighbours had not seen her for some days. When I went to report at the police at six in the evening, it struck me that she had not reported for some time. I was asked whether I knew what happened to her, but I had no knowledge.

We had to appear in court again. My colleague had seemingly fled the country. The gentleman who was with us, however, was told that he was actually missed during the coup raids and therefore he had to join other executive members in jail. The state had no case against me. I crossed to Harare with a valid passport and there was no sign of any threats of a second coup which the state alleged I had promoted. I was therefore set free. But, more was to come.

During the Christmas season of December '89, I was sleeping one night and thought I was sweating as it was a very hot night. Waking up in the morning, I accidentally glanced at my nightdress and found it had blood spots on it, especially on the left hand side. I examined myself and realised that it was actually blood from the nipple of my left breast. The next night the same thing happened.

After Christmas I consulted the doctor who gave me a referral letter to Ga-Rankuwa hospital. On the 2nd of January 1990, a specimen was taken from my left breast. I had to return after a fortnight to get the results from the laboratory. The results were positive. I had breast cancer, which was in its second stage.

I had to be counselled while I lay in hospital. The only sensible option would be a mastectomy. I had a problem, which I could not come to terms with. Losing part of your body is like losing a best friend. But with time I became reconciled.

There are several causes of breast cancer, but the only one that could match my lifestyle was stress. I had just been released from prison, and I had just gone through a stressful court case.

Sometime in February of 1990, I underwent the mastectomy. When the breast had finished draining, I was sent home for a fortnight for it to heal. The next stage was chemotherapy. After each session of therapy I would return home.

Chemotherapy was the worst medical experience I had ever had. A week before treatment I'd be seriously ill in bed at the mere thought of it. After this I'd be nauseous, and suffer stomach cramps. The thought of food alone made me vomit. But I had to go through a number of such treatments.

After the chemo I was readmitted for radiotherapy. We slept at Ga-Rankuwa and every morning we were taken by bus to what was then H. F. Verwoerd Hospital. My schedule comprised one daily visit for the next three weeks. If for some reason you missed a day along the way, you had to start the three-week cycle afresh.

At that time, the nurses' strike for better working conditions and salaries took effect all over the country. Ga-Rankuwa Hospital was also affected. Support staff stayed away. The hospital was dirty; there were bloody clothes everywhere; patients had no change of clothes. The hospital smelt badly. There were no cooks. Visitors afraid of the strike could not bring us food. The army was called in to prepare meals. They fried large chunks of steak and bread. In the end those patients who could walk were sent home, on the understanding that they would be alerted by phone when the hospital returned to normal.

I stayed home for two weeks before being called back. Those of us who were on radiotherapy had to start from the beginning. When I measure the period I stayed in hospital from February, it added up to three months. I was ultimately discharged in April. That was not all. I still had to submit to regular check-ups, and I would have to take Tamoxifen regularly so as to contain the cancer.

By law I was still employed by Tlhabane College of Education. From my arrest in June 1988 up to the time I went to hospital my salary was paid regularly in the bank.

While at home after my operation, I had the chance of visiting the officials of the circuit, weak as I felt, informing them that my case ended in acquittal but that I was then still sick and would be in hospital for some time. I requested leave forms. The Inspector, Mr. Moeketsi informed me that an official from head office phoned the college telling them that Mrs. Bopalamo had been acquitted by the courts, and that she was free to resume duty. A letter to that effect was sent to the circuit office.

Then followed another call directing that the first information be ignored pending a letter from the Minister of Education.

I was at home two days before going back to hospital when the said letter was delivered personally to me. I signed for it. It read:

*"You are hereby dismissed from the employment of the*
*Department of Education with immediate effect."*

The Secretary for Education, Mr. Molosiwa had signed it. No reasons were advanced. Before going back to hospital, I informed my lawyers by phone. There was very little to be done until my treatment was complete.

All this time, my husband was serving a three-year prison sentence at Rooigrond. I was staying at home in Phokeng with my ailing mother. I had to maintain my daughter who was not working and her three children. My youngest son was still at University. When I look back, I can only wonder at God's miracles. Just how did I cope?

There were some notable persons who stood solidly by me during this difficult period. Bishop Kevin Dowling procured a Lawyer for Human Rights, Mr. David Bam, to assist in the recent dismissal case. In the end we had to give up. President Mangope had obviously intervened in the judicial process. Justice would not be forthcoming.

Being now unemployed, I started making applications to schools out beyond the boundaries of Bophuthatswana, the nearest being the Republic of South Africa. But, names of teachers banned in Bophuthatswana had been blacklisted and widely circulated. My name appeared on the list.

The Catholic college of education at Mogwase, Mankwe Christian College was opening in 1991. My application for a teaching post was turned down on the pretext that there were no posts available. The college was a partnership between the Bophuthatswana government and the Catholic Church. The only assistance they offered me was to allow me to run the college tuck-shop.

The first supply of stock was provided for me. The business was doing well indeed. But I soon discovered that I was being followed by strange cars, obviously those of the Special Branch. I would leave home early in the morning and come back late. The car I used was unreliable for I would sometimes get a breakdown on the lonely roads at night. I had to use different routes to avoid mysterious people who trailed me all the time.

One morning as I entered the gates of Mankwe Christian College, the security man gave me contact numbers of someone who urgently wanted to talk to me. His name was also given, but I could not recall it in my list of acquaintances. I phoned the number, and was told that the particular person was not on duty that day. Curiosity forced me to enquire into the whereabouts of this mysterious person. It was a police station.

Before this incident, three Bophuthatswana ministers had come to my tuck-shop. I served them like I would any customer, but already I sensed trouble. This visit and the phone number of an unknown person from the police station worried me. The day after I phoned the police station, I was called to meet a visitor in the students' dining room. He introduced himself to me and stated the purpose of his visit.

This was a man with a mission. He was sent to request me to co-operate with the police in identifying comrades, and in spying on their meetings and conferences. Nor did he come empty handed. My remuneration would be handsome. Furthermore I would be reinstated in my post at Tlhabane College of

Education, and would be allowed to run my tuck-shop as usual. He would be sorry indeed if I did not accept such a generous package.

As the students were already crowding in for lunch, he departed promising to see me again the next day.

I left the tuck shop earlier than usual that day. I had to see Bishop Kevin Dowling and relate to him what happened, for I relied on his sound advice. As expected, he advised me that he would be present at the meeting with my police agent. But then after consulting Mr. Bam, the human rights lawyer, he changed his mind, and came up with a very different strategy. They would rather supply me with a tape recorder, and instead of meeting the police agent at Mankwe Christian College, I should invite him to my house in Phokeng.

The tape was placed in an ordinary briefcase, which I kept slightly open on the table while he spoke and quizzed me. He revealed to me that only three people would know about our secret deal: the head of Special Branch, the President, and himself. My job would entail attending all meetings of the ANC. I would be supplied with transport, booked into the most expensive hotels, and carry substantial pocket money. My job would be to provide feedback and names of important personalities at such meetings.

Still my response was negative. The proposed task would be difficult to execute; more seriously, the plot being altogether incompatible with my moral values, was against my conscience, I explained.

However, he would not take no as a final answer; he persisted. He promised to come again. That was a Thursday, whilst my mother was preparing to go to her regular prayer meeting. He offered my mother a lift. In the meantime, I phoned the bishop to collect the briefcase and take it to the lawyers. The tape would form part of the court debates as we had started to engage the government legally for my re-instatement in Tlhabane College of Education.

The gentleman from the police soon got tired of me. After a week, the priest who had invited me to run the tuck-shop at Mankwe approached me with some pertinent news. A letter had been received by the rector of the college that I was to terminate my activities in the tuck-shop with immediate effect. The letter was from the Secretary for Education. I asked the priest what he thought I should do. He replied: "I think you should leave."

I packed the stock that was left in the tuck shop and headed home. It was clear that the president had declared war on my family and me.

As I visited the office of the Council of Churches in Rustenburg, I met one pastor who advised me to try a college at the then Kwa-Ndebele Homeland, presently Mpumalanga Province. This was Ndebele College of Education. In due course, I was called for an interview which proved successful. I would teach Communicative English to secondary student teachers.

Coming from a big house with ample accommodation, I now had to move into a single room with three of my grandchildren We used it as a bedroom, a kitchen and dining/sitting room. Fortunately we had a bathroom. My mother could not join us as I was not sure where and how she would be accommodated. It broke my heart to have to part with her. I was forced to take her to my sister's. She begged me to fetch her as soon as I had found the right accommodation.

Our accommodation constituted part of the girls' residence. The noise was unbearable but the girls were really wonderful. They just adored my grandchildren and were ready to assist us as much as possible. In the afternoon when the kids did their homework, they resorted to the foyer, noisy though it was. There some students would volunteer to assist them. On discovering that I was a fugitive from the Bop regime they showed much sympathy and understanding.

The language of the campus was mainly Isi-Zulu which I had little knowledge of. This forced me to speak English most of the time. But I was surprised one day nearing examinations when my classes called me to delimit the important sections of the syllabus for them. This was to assist them to focus on the essentials. On this particular day they spoke Sotho. I realised from that day onwards that when they wanted to, they could speak Sotho. However, they were not prepared to compromise their mother tongue for my sake. Only in a dilemma would they resort to it.

The staff comprised several nationalities but I was the only Motswana. There were quite a number of Zulu lecturers, a few Ndebeles and Northern Sothos, and many Afrikaners from Marble Hall. In the staffroom the Afrikaners sat by themselves, and ate together. The Blacks too kept together in the same way. What a segregated institution!

I was greatly attracted to Phindi, the only Swazi member of staff. She became everything to me. When I looked for better accommodation outside the college, Phindi helped willingly, and with no strings attached. She was aware that I was a foreigner and had few local connections. Soon she knew of my problems back home. I had to enrol my grandchildren at a very expensive school, Star of Hope, which was far from where we stayed. They would have struggled with Isi-Zulu. The Ndebele language was still under-developed, and lecturers at the college were just starting to standardise its spelling and grammar.

I used to enjoy my Sundays when I would go to the local Catholic Church where I was always welcomed. They already invited me to assist where I could in the running of the parish. Word also spread to other parishes, and they in turn, invited me to assist. They invited me as a speaker to motivate the youth. I was happy to be welcomed like that. Indeed in the eyes of Christ "there is neither Jew nor gentile; no male or female..." One of the lecturers at the College was a catholic and a lay preacher. He hailed from Durban.

Through Phindi's efforts I accessed better accommodation, though a little far from the college. Here I could have my own bedroom. The kids would have theirs. There was a kitchen- cum- sitting room, and a bathroom.

My son Kennedy had provided me with a car. The one I used had been a disaster, breaking down frequently in the middle of nowhere. He also supplied me with his old lounge suite and bedroom suite when he changed furniture. I brought three single beds from home, and so at last, we were comfortably accommodated.

The Ndebele people are well known for cleanliness and thrift. Even those who lived in shacks looked after their gardens diligently. Their gardens and lawns were always blooming with beautiful flowers and shrubs. You could hire someone on minimal payment and he/she would perform to your satisfaction. They are also creative, resourceful people who believe in self-reliance, rather than in buying.

For my three grandchildren, language was not going to be a handicap. They already spoke Ndebele. Ndebele was a spoken language only. The books at school, and even in church were in Zulu. Marble Hall was our nearest town but sometimes we drove to Groblersdal for better service.

A few weeks after arriving at the college in Siyabuswa, I went shopping in the evening in Marble Hall for that was the best time for shopping. Coming out of the supermarket, I must have slipped on some vegetable or fruit peals lying there and fractured my ankle. That was another crisis. Lying ill was the last thing I had expected. That night I lay awake with acute pain, waiting for daybreak. I was referred to hospital where a cast was applied. In college, my students were sympathetic and helpful. They were quick to carry my bag and books as I struggled with the stairs to my classes.

Later two young lecturers joined us. One, a lady had been a regular staff member and was now returning from maternity leave. The other, a man, was a new lecturer. The two soon became my best friends. It was to Phindi, Jane and Ncube that I confided my political persecution in Bophuthatswana. I made it clear to them that should Bophuthatswana be toppled, I would immediately pack up and return home with my grandchildren. So they became even more interested. We keenly followed political developments in Bop on a daily basis. This common concern formed us into a closely-knit group. I valued their friendship very much because generally I was ostracized. The Afrikaner lecturers, the rector and some of our black colleagues could never understand why I had ever got myself involved in politics in the first place.

I would drive home to Phokeng on most Friday afternoons, and would be back on Monday morning. Then I would drop the kids at Star of Hope School before driving on to the college. Whenever I was home, I would spend quality life with the church choir at St Joseph's to which I had taught several new hymns. I was always present to supervise my choir at events like the Blessing of the Oils during Holy Week. Choral music is balm to my soul.

By early 1994 it was plain to all that the political turmoil in Bophuthatswana was reaching its climax, despite President Mangope's propaganda that his country would survive for another 1000 years. A Setswana proverb advises, *Se sa feleng se a tlhola* (everything comes to an end). I had been watching the events with my friends at the college keenly anticipating the end when the homeland was finally toppled in April 1994.

I resumed contacts with head office at Mafikeng and explained my fate. I applied for a post and in August 1994 I was appointed circuit education officer of Rustenburg schools. Later in 1995 my position changed to district manager of education in Rustenburg. I was inaugurated and given offices in town. Ironically the offices I occupied were those of the former Transvaal Education Department (TED).

I faced my new post with a measure of apprehension. Part of my mandate was to co-ordinate the five education departments in the Rustenburg area: those of Bop, of the Coloureds, and of the Indian community; that of the Transvaal

Education Department (TED) for whites; and finally the Department of Education and Training (DET) for South African-based blacks.

My new office was staffed by former TED officials who amazed me with the genuine warmth of their welcome. Dr du Plessis graciously introduced me to the most spacious office in the whole building, the very one he himself was now vacating. He also indicated the beautiful new vehicle allotted to me for my official duties. Everything else was in keeping, and staff members excelled themselves in their competence and dedication. However, I noticed a tendency for some to quit their offices at about noon; of course I had to challenge this irregularity.

But not all groups were as co-operative as the exemplary TED staff members. Some former Bop officials found it difficult to adjust to the new dispensation and were inclined to drag their heels when asked to implement the many new initiatives. Similarly, many Bop principals still in their posts, who were so ready to accept "orders from above" just a year previously, now created our biggest administrative nuisance. They seemed to forget completely that negotiation is the best way to solve conflicts, and therefore they seemed ready to strike at the drop of a hat. Unfortunately some maintained their negative attitudes, despite our patient, diplomatic, pleading approach. Truth is, we enjoyed the authority to issue straight orders and insist on compliance, failing which we could have resorted to the ultimatum. This we opted not to do.

A peculiar case arose in the mainly Indian community of Zinniaville. There the principal of a school who described himself as a born-again Christian, insisted on displaying a religious picture in his office. He had resisted pleas from the school board to have the icon removed. Ultimately he resigned. Still in the context of religion, some Muslims pressed hard for their children to absent themselves from school at midday on Fridays so as to attend the mosque, but they too were refused.

Throughout my term in this Rustenburg post, I had to take disciplinary action against an official only once. The problem was absenteeism, which didn't stop even after confronting her several times. Actually, her trick was to place her bag prominently on her office table and abscond for the day; the impression being that she would return any minute! She even lodged a complaint at a party meeting in my absence, but a comrade intervened objecting that proceedings were irregular, since the defendant, me, was not present.

This women's excuse was that she was attending to her other official responsibilities. Finally, members of the ever-vigilant South African Democratic Teachers Union confronted me indignantly about this individual's ongoing absence. After an official investigation, she opted to resign.

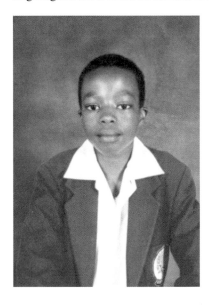

*Reabetswe grandson.*

Part Six

# Political
# Consciousness
# And Activism
# - SUNRISE

# The King Is Dead.
# Long Live The King!

◆

With the advent of democracy in 1994, the Truth and Reconciliation Commission (TRC), was instituted, and duly launched with much fanfare and great expectations. It was charged with the task of reconciling the former rulers and the ruled. Those who had abused their power by causing suffering in the form of imprisonment, torture, maiming, executions, or forced exile, would be given the chance to confess publicly to victims and their relatives, and in the process be granted pardon. Compensation was offered to victims and/or their relatives.

In Phokeng, where the fiercest battles against oppression by the homeland regime were fought, little reconciliation took place. As the result of this, people harboured hatred, bitterness and dissatisfaction for a long time. The TRC however, did hold a hearing at the Civic Centre in Phokeng but with the focus on Bafokeng concerns. At a hearing in Rustenburg, broadcast live on Radio Mafisa, a few victims came forward and broke the frightening culture of silence. But what measure of reconciliation was really effected in these TRC sessions amounted to just a drop in the ocean given the scale of human rights abuses in the former Bophuthatswana.

It was only later and behind their closed doors that aggrieved individuals in North-West province ventured to open their hearts about the offences perpetrated against them. They complained loudly of how the present authorities were doing nothing about them. At the funerals that I attended, those who were outspoken revealed these abuses publicly. I had the opportunity one day at a funeral of listening to a speaker taking his audience back to the bad days of the homelands. He mentioned how many suffered in prison; how others lost their jobs; how yet others were forced to flee their homes. Of course there were also those victims of assassinations, and those who died in unexplained "accidents". In this latter context, the name Mushi Bogopane springs to mind immediately. Mr Bogopane, a low-profile activist had been seriously harassed by the Bophuthatswana police. A brother-in-law to Rev Frank Chikane, then Secretary of the South African Council of Churches, Mushi was also a regular visitor to my home in Phokeng. Newly married, he had had to flee his home in Windsor, Phokeng, and take up residence in Rustenburg. He was ultimately killed in what is believed to be a contrived road accident.

Phokeng was the scene of acute and prolonged struggle precisely because the economic and political stakes were so high. Here we are dealing with the "platinum empire" and its emperor, Kgosi Edward Lebone Molotlegi. The president of Bophuthatswana wanted to dethrone the *kgosi* and replace him with his brother, George. Mangope could then gain much greater control of the land and its minerals. The percentage that was paid out to the Bophuthatswana government in the form of royalties from the platinum mines was apparently a larger sum than that paid to the tribe. The president therefore was accused of wanting to grab too much of the cake.

Those Bafokeng and others who fought against this injustice by the Bophuthatswana regime did not always have the luck of reaping the fruits of their struggle. In fact in many, many cases, the reverse occurred. The very ones who aided the regime in opposing Kgosi Edward were quick to come forward and be counted as honourable citizens of the "new South Africa".

On the other hand, some of those who paid the price during the struggle were doomed to remain behind as perpetual victims. They struggled to cope financially, emotionally, or even physically, and their problems escalated when yesterday's opponents became, overnight, their new leaders. These opportunists had managed somehow to run with the hare while hunting with the hound. From their new positions they controlled everything. As for the losers, they suffered subtle forms of discrimination in everything that was meant for the ordinary citizen. The true children of the struggle were left waiting at the end of the queue when they applied for jobs or bursaries.

Shakespeare's exclamation from the mob of his day, suits some of Mafikeng's new elite perfectly, "The king is dead. Long live the king!"

Translated, it reads, "Mangope is finished; Viva ANC! Viva!" Believe me, there were many peace-time heroes - and heroines.

But let's not generalize, and condemn *all* former Bophuthatswana civil servants and business persons as political opportunists. The truth is that the majority were competent in their posts and were persons of integrity. That they were capable of adapting to the new political order is very much to their credit. At times when politicians come and go and occasionally flags and other major symbols change, the public can look only to a capable and stable civil service. The newly established North West Province, headed by Premier Popo Molefe, depended on these former Bophuthatswana cohorts to deliver the essential services to new constituencies whose expectations were sky high. The premier was not disappointed.

In my view, the civil service of the then Bophuthatswana was more competent than that of today.

# Transition And Transformation

---◆---

After South Africa gained democracy in the general elections of 27<sup>th</sup> April 1994, the country had to transform. From the time the white man set foot in the Cape in 1652, the blacks had been under oppression. Three hundred years is a long period for anyone to re-adjust. Moreover, blacks had never voted before.

Before the elections of 1994, non-government organisations, churches and other volunteers went on a mission of teaching people what democracy meant and how to exercise their right to vote. They were free for the first time and freedom meant they could use their consciences to make their own decisions without fear of imprisonment. They were taught how to make a cross against the name of a leader they wanted.

Our form of ballot paper showed the names and pictures of party political leaders, and next to each picture was a block where you had to make a cross to vote for your preferred candidate.

It was not an easy exercise especially for blacks. Capital punishment was one of the worst laws during apartheid. Many, the majority of whom were blacks, were sent to the gallows erroneously as often, when cases were reviewed, the wrong person had died already. At least life sentence gives some chance to someone who had been found guilty by mistake of judgment. During appeal such judgment can be reversed.

Transformation is not easy. It cannot be achieved within ten or even 20 years. The present generation is lucky because they go to the same schools. They and their parents are beginning to realise that apartheid was after all, a senseless system that wasted time and resources! It has actually drawn the country years backwards. If the former South African authorities had listened to and heeded the words of Nelson Mandela and his colleagues, instead of incarcerating the charismatic leader for life on Robben Island, this country would not have wasted so much talent. Mandela and others could have turned the country around.

The present generation have the chance of living side by side. The fact that they were once divided along racial lines is now history. The present young parents have a role to play to rebuild this country where their children will live without seeing the next door child as an enemy because of the colour of their skin as in my childhood

I remember once during school holidays I visited my mother when she was employed at Sherwood Road in Johannesburg. I was only 13 or 14 years old. This place was just a few minutes walk from the Johannesburg Zoo. I visited the zoo to be entertained by the wild animals in cages, the birds, the reptiles and some marine animals. There were cement stools where we blacks rested when we tired of walking. Whites had proper seats under the trees. One day a friend, who also visited her mom for school holidays, accompanied me to the zoo. She came from Natal. Something just told us to sit on the lawn. It was green and quite comfortable like a new carpet. We sat and talked for a long time and did not notice a white security man approaching with a sjambok. Even if we had noticed, we would not have jumped; we were not committing any crime. Some white kids our age were also enjoying the comfort of the lawn. The security man did not utter a word to us; we just heard - and felt - the 'warp, warp' on our backs! We ran in different directions wondering what harm we had possibly caused. We left the zoo immediately fearing we might unwittingly draw some more trouble on ourselves. Blacks who witnessed this whipping were very sympathetic towards us - just two innocent kids.

Next time I accompanied the white children of my mother's employer to the same zoo. When we got tired, we sat on the same lawn, ate ice cream and other snacks. Nobody disturbed our peace. We were spotted by a security man but he did not even think of using his sjambok, which he held all the time. How little we Blacks complained at the time. Abuse had become the normal practice; yet it was so barbaric.

At the primary school I attended at Polonia, in 1953 there was this salute of raising a thumb backward and remarking *Africa mayibuye*! One afternoon a group of us children were returning from De Wildt shops on errands for our parents. Sometimes in company, teenagers can do silly things, which when alone, they would not dream of. One boy, our classmate, raised his thumb crying, *Mayibuye* and the group responded, 'Africa.' We did not notice our class teacher coming behind us on a bicycle. He had a tendency of cycling to the shops in the afternoons. On the carrier of his bicycle, he had usually a loaf of bread, and some butter and milk.

Those were luxuries most of our families could ill afford, except if our parents in Johannesburg sent them with transport that came our way on weekends. The drivers of these vehicles made extra money by frequenting our parents at their work places asking for anything they wanted to send their children back home every Saturday evenings. We waited patiently for the hooters outside. Then we would rush out and maybe carry boxes of nice dried slices of buttered bread, and dried cooked meat. These we called *dikokola*. My mom had a paper laid on the floor of her room. After breakfast, she took all the slices of bread left over, buttered them and laid them to dry. In the evening she did the same with the leftover meat.

The following day in school, our class teacher called us, and asked what we meant by *Africa Mayibuye*. We had no clue of what we meant. He then referred particularly to the boy whose thumb was raised and asked him whether he thought Africa would return when boys like him could not even button their shirts. Matthews was a bit careless about most things. Our class teacher would poke fun at the open shirt remarking that Mathews was selling his belly! On the particular morning he said to him, *"Africa e ka boa jang mo mothong yo o rekisang mogodu jaaka wena?"* The class laughed.

With older people, even though mock elections were repeatedly conducted in all areas of the country, mistakes still occurred. Some people mistook a cross to mean you do not prefer a person/leader when we counted, we discovered many such errors. The cross being placed directly on the head of a leader they disliked. Old people are like small children sometimes. They are very innocent. When they come out of the voting station they boast about whom they voted for and how they carried out the activity. They would boast that they scratched so-and-so's head (an enemy) with a cross, because they disliked them. As a result of such ignorance we had many spoilt ballots.

During the first elections of 1994 the African National Congress won with a huge majority.

The new South Africa had been divided into nine provinces, as a result of the talks at Kempton Park. In all the provinces the ANC won, except in KwaZulu-Natal, which had been embroiled in war with the ANC before elections. It had thus become a no-go area. Provincial elections meant every province would have its own premier, and its own parliament called the Provincial Legislature. The new provinces were KwaZulu-Natal, Western Cape, Eastern Cape, Northern Cape, Limpopo, Gauteng, North West, Free State and Mpumalanga. These replaced the four provinces Free State, Cape, Natal and Transvaal that came into being with the formation of the Union of South Africa in 1910.

It would appear that democracy education should have been continued even after the first elections were over. But very little was done. Even the media, print and electronic, which did much work in educating the public in 1994, did not assist anymore. This resulted in even worse errors than before and many people did not quite internalise democracy. The other error was that posters were written in English only. Not all voters could read them. It is only now that posters are written in all languages of the regions of South Africa.

Failure to internalise democracy make transformation even more difficult. Either people did not know their rights or they abused them. Children thought they had more rights than anyone else and some adults thought that children had no rights at all. Whereas in the past the stick was used in the classroom, after 1994 such punishment was abolished. Punishment with a cane was tantamount to assault and was declared a criminal act. Teachers were warned not to abuse their powers. The home too as a social institution had to be careful in the way it disciplined children.

Many cases of abuses of children and violence in families started to emerge. The number of these cases was a wake-up call to our society. This meant that these abuses had been going on unreported. Families have a tendency of sweeping evil acts under the carpet, warning members that they are domestic matters and are not for the public to know. We wonder how many children and spouses have lost heir lives in the privacy of their homes.

With democracy came transparency. South Africa is so transparent that even the president of the country can be hauled before a court of law. Nobody is above the law. The former State Presidents were effectively a law unto themselves. If you criticised the government of those years you could be detained under the Internal Security Act and held in solitary confinement. Today the government can be criticised or advised by the public on how best to rule the country. That is why the government goes around the country engaging the public in People's Forums. People get a chance of voicing their views and government takes them seriously.

The Equality Clause in the constitution means that all are equal. Probably this came into being because of past experiences. There were laws that governed white South Africans and another code that governed blacks.

The distinction of groups meant that every aspect of life was segregated. There were separate waiting rooms, separate toilets, separate institutions of learning, separate restaurants, separate carriages in trains. Even at work place these differences prevailed on a large scale. In one Rustenburg Mine, a black man was shot dead for using a cup that was meant for whites.

Black domestic workers raised their boss's children from childhood. They washed and fed them. When mealtime came, they had to eat outside using separate utensils. Even after preparing the meals, they commonly had a different menu from that of the household.

I used to visit my mother at her workplace during holidays. When meat was on the menu there was one type called "The Boys' Meat" which was ordered for my mother and the men working outside in the garden. Samp, beans and mielie meal formed the menu for these employees. No consultation was done with my mother when these grocery items were ordered. It does not mean she could not eat samp and beans, but it was only on rare occasions. They are not our stable food. But my mother rarely cooked it for herself. She always ate what she had prepared for her employer. She did not eat fish either. On Fridays the dish for the day was always fish and chips. She made the best fish and chips ever. When we were around during holidays we enjoyed fish and chips and always looked forward to Fridays. Sometimes instead of chips, she prepared mashed potatoes.

The equality law, however, is still a problem among many black South Africans, as it also influences the way men and women relate. In the past, as throughout the industrial world, men earned more than women doing similar jobs. This has changed. Men retired from work at age 65, while women had to retire at 55. Today they are free to retire at 65. Pregnant women could apply for maternity leave while their spouses could not. Today men can apply for their paternity leave when their kids are born.

What still remains a big misunderstanding in black cultures is the equality of married couples, and of partners who co-habit. Men cannot let go their "my word is final" or "I am the boss here" attitude. This is the main cause of family violence. Most men want to treat their spouse as domesticated second-class citizens. The woman must go to work at the same time as he does then she comes home to prepare meals, bathe the baby, wash dishes and see to it that everyone has clean clothes for work or school the next day. The husband rests, reads a newspaper, watches television, or even visit friends. Some of them never think for once what goes on in their partners' minds.

Yes, in some cases there are tough women who take advantage of this equality law to abuse their partners. But these are very rare cases. Most women are abused - physically, emotionally and economically.

The other unfortunately aspect of our culture, is the blame the society puts on a woman. When a family does not seem to have peace, it becomes "that woman from such and such a place" (your birthplace). When there are no children in a marriage there is an insulting term given to the women, *moopa, meaning* barren. Nothing is said of a man. When kids become boisterous, they have taken after the mother or her family. When they are brilliant and well mannered, the women do not receive the praise.

Consultation has never been part of life for many black families. The man dictates terms, he controls the purse, he calls a house his own, even if it was a joint effort. He can do whatever he likes in it, or with it. Rural women are the worst hit. But with the advent of democracy things are gradually changing. A woman can now lay a charge against an abusive husband. Black police are, however, also brought up in the same culture, and they will always dilly-dally before they apprehend the perpetrator. Sometimes they try to talk him out of this habit and leave him without arresting him. Some men have murdered their spouses only after police left, with the hope that they made peace. Men have an ego and reporting them to authorities sometimes infuriates them and makes them even more violent.

But there are exceptional men you can really admire, who treat their spouses like queens. These are real family men who feel for their wives and support them all the way. When they are sick they nurse them and they don't call on someone else, or leave the wife alone and helpless.

Life would be so pleasant if two people lived a happy, harmonious life, feeling for, supporting, and loving each other. That would be such a good example to set for growing children. Children would build sound families and raise good citizens. Problems in our schools today are the outcome of family backgrounds.

Another aspect of our democracy, which many find problematic, is criminals' rights. In the past before a person was tried in a court of law, just the mere suspicion that one had perpetrated a crime left one open to severe assault. Because blacks did not know their rights, they would not even lay a charge of assault against police officers. The debate today however, focuses on victims' rights.

# Long, Lonely Road

---◆---

In my life as a teacher, I have taught at all levels of education. I have worked in most classes through primary school, and actually once taught Grade Ones. At post-primary levels, I have taught in junior secondary, and high school as far as matric classes. I have also lectured in two colleges of education.

I have filled the role of Chief Circuit Education Officer and that of District Manager of Education.

At a certain point I felt that I needed a change. Coming back from KwaNdebele, I started engaging actively once again with the African National Congress (ANC) at both regional and branch levels. I was elected secretary to both.

In 1999, when the list for Parliamentarians was drafted, my name appeared. I was then elected to the Provincial Legislature of North West Province.

Immediately I was requested to serve as the chairperson of the Education Portfolio Committee. Members of legislatures serve in several portfolio committees even if they act as chairperson of one. Thus, as chairperson of the Education Portfolio Committee, I also served in the committees of Public Works, Transport, Agriculture, Local Government and Housing, Safety and Liaison, and also Public Accounts. There were *ad hoc* committees in which I served in human resource development.

Different political parties form parliament or the legislature. These parties are represented in all portfolio committees. The majority party always holds the largest representation. One, two or three MPs may represent smaller parties. These smaller parties face a major challenge in parliament. They tend to be over- stretched in their efforts to attend as many meetings as possible, and to collect and collate important information.

In a portfolio committee, such as that of education, a host of issues and problems are raised for discussion. Information is obtained by occasionally inviting officials of the Department of Education, to report on matters such as buildings, renovations, staffing, school discipline, involvement of parents, exam results, electricity, water supply, adopt-a-cop, and how the department deals with HIV/AIDS. We also pass budgets, and investigate how the budget was used, or why it was not used as intended.

We found it unwise to depend solely on any one department as there was a noticeable tendency to present as rosy a picture as possible and in doing so to hide some of the shortcomings.

The Portfolio Committee must then make arrangements to visit the relevant institutions so as to access first hand information. Sometimes we obtain information that is unknown to department officials who have been negligent in carrying out constant and proper monitoring and reporting.

From our side we would then discuss our findings with the department and advise them on which areas needed attention. In normal situations, this is the right approach to governance and delivery of services. But there were departments or rather MECs who felt threatened by such oversight reports; officials appeared embarrassed and tended to become defensive.

As chairperson of a portfolio committee and a member of other committees, I talk straight and call a spade a spade, without having "to buy anybody's face". My conviction was that I was helping both the department and the party to grow. I never at any time thought of challenging the integrity of my comrades in the executive. Yet as a member of the same party, I had the obligation to present the true picture of conditions at schools, or on roads or at Public Works projects, and thus prod some comrades to pull up their socks. When I entered parliament I was no longer young. My life experience, my educational status and my inter-personal skills have all taught me to stand on principle. To me the truth is sacred and cannot be compromised.

I was scarcely aware, however, of the damage, and worse of all, the ostracising I was suffering. Obviously I had ruffled many feathers. As I reflected later on the whole parliamentary scene I concluded that this game which is politics is best suited to young people; especially the docile types who take dictation from their crafty seniors and suppress their own moral feelings. But where would such parliamentarians lead our country, except deeper into trouble?

I never resorted to publishing our mistakes in the media, as the Opposition would do. But that did not stop me from standing up in Parliament and pointing out mistakes. Of course I also recognised achievements and very often commended the Department of Education when the occasion merited it.

Portfolio committees employ administrators whose duty is to arrange meetings and oversight visits. These administrators arrange where you will be accommodated for the night; where you will have your meals; how many schools you will visit per day and who you will meet; how long it takes to drive from point A to B; and who are the local authorities to be invited so that you don't do oversights alone. These latter had to be witnesses to our findings.

Portfolio committees have support staff who accompany them. Their immediate task is to prepare a room or hall where a meeting will take place and put recording machines in place.

At the end of a meeting the portfolio administrator prepares a report which the chairperson proof reads and corrects. The report is re-edited before it is distributed to members of the committee. He/she then finds a slot in the parliamentary schedule where the report can be discussed and adopted.

The committee next decides whether the Department of Education should be summoned to respond to the contents of the report, or whether it should be taken to the House, or both.

It is not always the case that the Opposition is visible in committee meetings. But when a report goes to the House for debate, then members of the Opposition criticise the department through the MEC, for failure or negligence. They have this right.

Opposition politics does not necessarily mean we are enemies. It merely shows different people with different approaches to life and therefore different points of view. Opposition politics should be constructive. After all, members of the Opposition are part of the society in which we all live. Like MPs of the ruling party, they must reflect the views and priorities of their respective constituencies. Opposition politics is the very backbone of democracy.

When I entered parliament I realised that the work pattern was different from that of my previous experiences. Previously my work was organized and predictable. Even if changes occurred they would seldom be unmanageable.

But for parliamentarians the change of pace - or the pace of change - can be devastating. You are required to be available 24 hours a day, 7 days per week. You must be all things to all people, as well as being the ultimate problem solver. Public expectations are often unrealistically high. Worst of all you must be an expert fire fighter. If a school suddenly goes on strike, or a child is expelled for reasons not compatible with the constitution, or the South African School Act, the portfolio committee chairperson must rush to the scene to gain first hand information, and establish the facts. Imagine this scenario: You are called to a school building site where work was suddenly abandoned when the foundations were laid. Probing deeper, you learn that the contractor had been paid the full amount in advance, and that he has now "vanished without a trace". You take the issue to the portfolio committee meetings. Finally you are advised to abandon the matter altogether! You ask yourself if this is what our protracted national struggle has produced.

Every day invitations inundate your desk. Some of these you cannot afford to ignore. In short, MPs work under enormous stress. At no time must a member make himself or herself unavailable by closing a phone. Even at midnight you could be ordered to depart at dawn for Cape Town or Gauteng or Mpumalanga - or even abroad. You have to comply.

Your main responsibility as a politician is to those voters who elected you to parliament in the first place. You must represent them in all major matters. If you absent yourself from duty, you show little respect for the constituency that is looking to you to improve their lives. You travel early and late on remote routes day in, day out, running from one outpost to the next, trying to solve this problem or that. The pace is such that you have little or no chance to make a proper follow up, so you feel quite nervous returning to the school with the original problem. You only hope and pray that they have implemented your recommendations.

As politicians, we were also expected to attend all gatherings, rallies, people's forums, meetings, conferences and any other activity of the party. We were charged exorbitant levies at these meetings, more than any other person present. We also paid our party levy to the provincial office as well as to the national office. When you add together what parliamentarians have to spend over and above personal allowances, you realise that they actually receive a relatively meagre salary. Think too of vehicle maintenance. Your vehicle is exposed to very bad roads on many occasions, and you bear the costs of repairs. Added to all these is your health which is under tremendous strain on a daily basis.

Besides routine portfolio committee business, political parties also engage in serious study and research. Study groups are established to scrutinize new bills in accordance with the party's policies. In these groups there are resource persons who can interpret policies, or lecture the group on any aspect that is not clear. Study groups also look at sensitive matters that may be raised in the House by the Opposition and find ways in which to deal with them. If deemed necessary, the group may invite an expert from outside to update it on a pressing issue.

In parliament I also chaired the study group for social transformation. This group is made up of politicians who serve in portfolio committees of education, health, public works, agriculture and social welfare. The MECs of these departments also serve as members of the study group. Heads of departments and other office bearers of the party are members. The secretary of the study group may come from outside parliament as provided by the office of the particular party.

Parliament used to sit once a week, on Tuesday. Parliamentarians on such days try to look presentable. I enjoyed these sittings very much because I always participated in the debates. I would have my speech prepared well in advance so as not to be caught napping.

Parliamentarians are also exposed to workshops in order to widen their mental horizons. Some of us were even enrolled for a diploma in MBA studies. When I terminated my term in parliament I was left with one module to complete this course. We were also supplied with laptops and received training on how to operate them.

One of my main problems was trying to cope with the volume of information which came to us in print form. You had to familiarise yourself with it to remain ahead at meetings and debates. Every morning you'd find your table covered with information documents, reports, letters, and invitations. One secretary served about four parliamentarians. It was therefore a problem for him or her to update us on the business of the day while attending to other tasks.

The Chief Whip looks after the interest of his/her party members. You report to him/her if you are indisposed and cannot attend sittings of parliament. He/she then announces your apology in the House. He/she may refuse permission, or grant it, or even refuse an apology that does not sound authentic.

Majority opinion tended to pre-empt the need for serious analysis of the most sensitive moral issues. In such an environment you easily compromise your individual freedom as you are compelled to go with the flow. The best you could do was to remain quiet rather than sound negative.

Even with ordinary colleagues when discussing issues generally affecting the party, you had to be careful with your remarks. Some things you said innocently to those you regarded as friends might reach those in power. You were not given the chance to explain why you said what you said; you just felt the negative vibes which hurt a lot. I also came to realise that at the National Assembly things were better - there parliamentarians enjoyed their democratic rights much more than we did in the legislatures. The worst experience was when information meant for you, was withheld. Yet another bitter pill was the animosity displayed among members of the same party. This was so pronounced that even the Opposition would remark on it.

Towards the end of my term in parliament I felt my health was no longer robust enough to continue. All too frequently I found myself in and out of hospitals. My conscience would no longer give me rest as I always felt guilty when for health reasons I had to be absent from this or that meeting. I kept asking myself whether it was worthwhile attempting to carry on. I was always troubled. But how would I otherwise maintain the family that looked up to me for its survival?

When my party was organizing, and mobilising people for the elections of 2004, my health was in a very bad state. Sometimes when you are unwell, party members think you feign illness, especially during elections. In truth I was very ill. I had come back from Sandton Medi Clinic for a lumbar manipulation. I was told there was nothing that could be done to my back unless I lost between 25 or 30 kilograms. I found it difficult to sit for a long-time, to stand, or to walk a long distance. Sleeping was more a torture than anything else. I had to do exercises in bed every night in the hope of catching some sleep.

My doctor attempted to put me on a weight-loss programme. When I lost sixteen kilograms, I looked terrible. I could not even look myself in the mirror, but the back pain got better.

While I was struggling with my back, my left shoulder gave in, and had to be operated upon. I was home for a week and half and the sutures were due to be removed the next week when I suddenly I fell ill. The pain in the stomach was unbearable. I vomited many times. I had to be admitted to hospital as an emergency. Ex-rays were taken, and sonar was also done. The result: intestinal obstruction. An emergency operation was done within twenty-one hours.

Before all these ailments beset me, I had been going for regular physiotherapy of the back. Now I had to do physiotherapy of the shoulder instead.

It is said that political careers begin with cheers, but end with tears. This was not the case with me. I had got my fill of life in the parliamentary fast lane, which to me was a killing rate-race. I had exhausted myself on the long, lonely roads of North West Province, often in fruitless - and thankless  trips that become merry-go-rounds. It all exacted a terrible price on my health. I had had enough! Anyway, were there not better ways of serving my people?

# Trips Abroad: So Near, And Yet So Far

◆

In 1986, a group representing the Bafokeng Women's Club of which I was a member visited Malawi. That was during the regime of President Kamusu Banda. The president seemed revered by young and old. The Malawians are a simple and accommodative nation. Most of the hotels we visited and business places employ men. We always asked ourselves where the women folk were. But as we drove through the countryside, we saw women grinding maize in stumping blocks. Sometimes we passed women on the way with children on their backs, loads on their heads and other children walking beside and behind them. They walked long distances. At one kraal, we went round hoping to see women. Only when we went deeper did we come upon old women sitting alone behind huts. We gained the impression that the country was seriously underdeveloped, and this impression was reinforced by the absence of women from the workplace.

Malawian women are very trim and slim. During the days I spent there, I did not see an overweight person like we find in South Africa. The men working in hotels are good cooks. They do the washing for guests and are very reliable.

Our visit coincided with Malawi's independence celebrations. We were invited to the stadium where all the activities took place. The colourful traditional attire worn by Malawian women was amazing. When Kamusu Banda entered the stadium there was ululating. He held a horsetail, white in colour, which he waved from side to side. He rode horse-drawn cart which was followed by an entourage of black Mercedes-Benz vehicles. Before they were seated on the stage, the national anthem was sung and everything came to a standstill. Even outside the stadium the walking, hawking, and talking stopped. Hush, but this was the silence of fear. Banda was a dictator.

We were also impressed by the performance of a youth group, *The Born Free*, even though they were anything but free! They are the youth who were born after Malawi gained independence from the British.

At some point during the celebrations, the women in their multi-coloured attire danced in a circle at the centre of the stadium. Then Kamusu Banda would descend from the stage with his white *seditse* and enter the circle formed by the women. It was quite impressive seeing him point at the groups in turns - they would then come and dance beautifully in front of their president. The singing was excellent and we appreciated the occasion.

In June 1990 the Women Ministries of the South African Council of Churches, sent me and a colleague from the Northern Province, Mrs Modiba, as delegates to Switzerland. Our assignment was to conscientise women's groups on the plight of South African women at the time. We were guests of the Swiss Federation of Christian Women.

The year 1990 was a period when many political prisoners were released. South Africa was at the time gearing itself to receive those who had fled the apartheid regime. We were also looking forward to the unbanning of political organisations, the release of Nelson Mandela, the Conference for a Democratic South Africa (Codesa), and the dawn of the New South Africa.

It was a very difficult period indeed. There was war which the regime alleged was between the Zulus of Inkatha and the ANC. Worse still, it was blacks fighting blacks. In actual fact, it was a war perpetrated by the regime against the ANC, and was used to distract the country's attention from the all-important "talks about talks" for the formation of the new South Africa. These wars caused deaths in Soweto, KwaZulu-Natal and many parts of the country.

The Swiss women gave us a warm welcome. We came out of winter in South Africa and arrived in their summer, which was not that different from our winter. Having been advised that it was summer there, we packed only light clothes. However, they were kind enough to give us sweaters. They also bought us walking shoes. In Europe they do a lot of walking - to do shopping, catch buses, and to board trains. They walk long distances; unlike in South Africa, where people use cars for even short distances. In Swiss towns, the only cars we saw were those used by very high officials. The intention is to minimise air pollution. The Swiss are health conscious and their cities are spick and span. I found the landscapes inspiringly beautiful.

We were accommodated by Dorothea, one of our hostesses. There was already a programme for each of us when we arrived. Our main task was to update the different groups about the new developments in our country. They wanted to know why blacks were killing one another. The idea of the Third Force remained quite incomprehensible to them, no matter how much we explained. The other lady who worked hand in hand with our hostess was Mrs Wolftard. We dined at her house several nights, on meals prepared by her husband.

We visited Geneva, Zurich and many parts of Switzerland. We also found time to row across the River Rhine and climb part of the Alps. Although it was summer, the mountain was still covered with snow and I noted what I had so often seen in photographs: the melting snow had formed streams which flowed into the river.

While in Switzerland, I had to prepare for another tour which was to take me to Eastern Europe. In this trip, I was representing women through the South African Council of Churches (SACC) and was among pastors selected from different church groups around the country.

En route to Eastern Europe, we participated in a *Pax Christi* conference in Amsterdam where the topic was North-South relationships: how impoverished the South was and what the North could do to resolve this problem. It was a multi-lingual conference facilitated by simultaneous translations. We spent a night here. The next day we flew to East Berlin. We met a few organisations there. Our brief was to listen to East Berliners as they shared their hopes for re-union and reconciliation with their neighbours in West Berlin. This we did as we were anticipating changes in South Africa. We did not want to repeat the mistakes committed after World War II where Germans did not have the chance of addressing their psychological wounds.

From East Berlin we moved on to Prague, Czechoslovakia, and then to Poland. We were interested in how these countries were managing their recent transition from Communism. I focused on how these changes affected women and children.

We visited Auschwitz and Warsaw concentration camps. In Warsaw we saw a group of young Israeli people who were praying and crying bitterly as if the wars between Hitler against their Jewish nation happened the previous day. It was then that we realised that no effort at reconciliation and healing had ever been attempted. While speaking to organisations and individuals we came upon those who were still emotionally affected by the events of 50 years ago. Our trip ended at West Berlin.

How economically different we found the West and the East. Although the Berlin Wall had been dismantled, the psychological discrimination still existed. The East complained that the West was looking down upon them.

I had the opportunity again in 1995 of visiting Eastern Europe for the same purpose. The Institute for Contextual Theology (ICT) had initiated this trip. In Poland we were accommodated in Polonia House. Yes, the Polonia of my childhood! It was here I discovered the meaning of the name.

In Poland I also had the opportunity of visiting the Church of the Black Madonna. Tourists visit this church in great numbers on a daily basis. Mass is celebrated throughout the day and the congestion is such that you have to hold hands so as not to lose your companions.

In the year 2000 while in parliament I joined an education portfolio committee from the NCOP (National Council of Provinces). This committee had invited education portfolio committee chairpersons from all provinces to accompany them to India and Malaysia on a study tour. The NCOP is the Second Chamber of the National Parliament and acts as a House of Review. It also the constitutional link between the National Assembly and Provincial Parliaments.

Our trip started at the Johannesburg airport and we flew non-stop to Singapore airport - a clinically clean, vast, state-of-the-art facility. However, this was only a stop-over en route to India. The airport at New Delhi provided a near-total contrast to that of Singapore; it was hot, humid, noisy and dirty.

Arriving at New Delhi we were introduced to the High Commissioner of South Africa in India. He impressed me as being highly competent, accommodative, and helpful, and his face was always full of smiles. We had a warm welcome in his official residence. Our first official meeting was with him and he briefed us about India and the designated spots we were going to visit.

As we moved about the sprawling city, we experienced grinding poverty first hand. Whenever our bus stopped we were swarmed with beggars, young and old. They even went as far as climbing on the bonnet of our vehicle, knocking on the windscreen with empty hands asking for whatever. At a certain store where we stopped to look at the jewellery, I was the last person to reach the bus when a woman with an infant caught up with me. She begged me to take the child in exchange for money. She had nothing to eat she told me. I was shocked and alarmed. The whole incident overwhelmed me.

Neither in India nor in Malaysia could we engage in really open discussions. Issues like teenage pregnancy, HIV/AIDS, prostitution, could not even be mentioned, still less honestly discussed. In stark contrast we told them about our problems in South Africa but still they denied having any social problems at all! I realised while in Malaysia that our democracy in South Africa has been stretched very far, to the extent that our transparency is close to nakedness. Perhaps that is why other countries have the perception that our crime rate is so high.

In Malaysia for instance, at the world's highest twin tower, I was robbed of my wallet which contained cash and all my bankcards and my cell phone was stolen from my room. These incidents contradicted the official line; there is no crime in Malaysia!

In Nairobi, Kenya, where we attended the Commonwealth Parliamentary Association Conference, we met with different delegates from African countries and shared our African experiences. We South Africans speak very good English but our weakness is ignorance of French spoken so fluently in West Africa, and of Portuguese spoken in Mozambique and Angola.

Malaysia is a predominately Islamic country; Kenya is less so.

In London unlike Geneva, many cars can be seen on the streets but the high officials use taxis. People prefer walking. We had talks with MPs in their portfolio committee of Public Accounts and enjoyed the experience we gained. We discovered that Britain has a problem of truancy in their schools, but there the police have to be involved. Police officers monitor shopping malls and accompany truant scholars back to school.

We were happy to visit London Eye on the River Thames, Buckingham Palace, and parts of the countryside. We were also entertained at South Africa House in Trafalgar Square. Our one problem was shopping. With an exchange rate of R12 to the Pound, we had to limit our purchases to just a few books.

When South Africa House invited us for a *braai*, we were all excited and in mouth-watering anticipation of pap and beef steak. But what a fiasco! Instead of pap we were served white bread rolls, and in place of beef they dished up barbequed chicken from Nandos.

My travels included a visit to Bray, which though geographically close to us is perhaps as foreign as any European country I've visited. Bray is perched on the sandy Namibian border - it is a place in the middle of nowhere where the former South African Government settled Koevoet soldiers. These soldiers had been posted at this remote frontier for a purpose. During the critical period leading up to 1994, they were used as mercenaries in the notorious Third Force. They were engaged in military campaigns in KwaZulu Natal and elsewhere that were falsely labelled by Pretoria's public relations departments as black on black conflict. Koevoet activities deepened the rift between Inkatha and the ANC and to that extent seriously hampered the delicate Codesa negotiations that were paving the way for the new dispensation.

At Bray we stayed at a bush guest house. The sand in the area is so deep that our official vehicle got stuck and we therefore had to summon transport from Vryburg. A sign at the gate of the guest house reads: "Beware of Elephants".

We got out -it was late at night and we had to wade knee-deep in the sand while peeping nervously over our shoulders for wandering elephants. Luckily, we didn't have far to walk.

The next day we held a meeting with this community of former Koevoet families. They still cannot speak any of our languages, so we had to engage an interpreter. That's how foreign Bray is.

There is a primary and a high school in the area. For years not a single government official had visited them. The failure rate in the schools is very high and discipline is close to zero. Teachers and learners turn up at school at odd hours, and sometimes they miss each other completely!

They have to walk a distance of about 80km to reach the nearest Health Centre. Their problems were enormous.

But Bray is foreign in yet another way. Members of the South African Police Services accompanied us on this visit and one of the officers cautioned me: "If the government delays bringing services to these people, we might experience problems." I agree. As mostly unemployed mercenaries, these guys are vulnerable, and any new mischievous agent could recruit them for whatever cause. The officer confided to us that these veterans still had easy access to dangerous weapons. Officially of course, they had been instructed to surrender all their guns a long time back, but what real guarantee is there that all weapons had been turned in? Bray is near, and yet so far.

As members of the Safety and Liaison Portfolio Committee, we received serious complaints of stock theft. In the presence of the police, farmers alleged that stock theft was on the increase. Perpetrators are not apprehended because they allegedly connive with the police. This was the outcry in almost all communities we visited. Like hijacked cars, cattle were said to be driven across national borders, and one old man reported boastfully, but with some satisfaction, that he had traced some of his herd all the way to Botswana.

Transformation is not easy. No matter how much we talk about it, implementation remains the only test. When all is said and done, there is much more said than done!

As a Member of Parliament in the North West Province, I have visited almost all parts of the territory: Rustenburg, Koster, Swartruggens, Madikoe, Kuruman, Vryburg, Taung, Lichtenburg, Coligny, Potchestroom, Klerksdorp, Wolmaranstad, Bloemhof, Christiana, Brits, Derby, Morokweng, and Pampierstad.

Part Seven

# Oh!
# For A Second
# Liberation

# Education
# Liberation For Moral Life

◆

Today, children are not coerced into studying Religious Education. It has been dropped from school syllabi. Children however need moral guidance to help them exercise their rights. I believe that Religious Education (RE) made a valuable contribution in the character building of children and now it is a pity that it is discontinued, no alternative such as ethics has replaced it. The absence of RE in schools will have adverse effects on society's morals especially if the programme of moral regeneration promoted by the government does not work.

Parents are the first teachers of their children. Apart from Church Schools, where children received religious education, the secular education system in which most children are educated has left parents unsupported. How many parents today realistically have time to teach children about God without help from others? Many parents leave home before dawn and return at dusk, tired out after a day's work to find their children asleep. They have little enough time to prepare for the next day.

Churches have traditionally helped the parents in their task as religious educators. Often parishioners only meet on Sunday. In some cases children may for example attend confirmation classes after school during the week. Many in society no longer regard religion as important, and parents do not see to it that children attend these classes regularly while children often arrive late for class or absent themselves. We are raising a generation with little regard for religion. On the other hand, although the role of certain churches was very influential, many within the churches supported apartheid while others produced men and women with strong moral values.

Apartheid confused many as to the purpose of religion as those who framed and implemented the laws of separation were religious people who believed the Bible taught that blacks were not equal with them in the sight of God.

Immediately after political liberation people began meetings without prayer. The reason or excuse was that South Africa is a multi-religious country. Whose prayer was to be said? Later South Africa religious diversity was taken into account in a positive way, and diverse religious leaders were invited to lead meetings in prayer. The Bill of Rights in the Constitution of the Republic of South Africa encourages this practice.

*Maggie at Bethel Practising School with a group of Sunbeams.*

# Cultural Diversity Opportunities And Constraints On Liberation

◆

Many of our children in South Africa now attend multiracial schools. In this process they encounter children of diverse cultures and make friends with them. Parents however, need to be aware that children need a lot of support in this environment if they are to retain respect for their culture of origin. It is natural for children to want to emulate the attractions of cultures other than their own. This may lead to changes in behaviour that parents find unacceptable, and this in turn may lead to confrontation and confusion as parents find it difficult to accept changes in children's patterns of behaviour. But does speaking English change a person into an Englishman or woman? Education in a pluralist culture inevitably changes South African society. Rather than resist change it is advisable for parents to recognise they are part of the processes willingly or unwillingly. This of course does not mean that children should not be fluent in their mother tongue and have a deep appreciation of their proper culture, traditions, and values.

Some cultural practices in today's South Africa are time consuming and conflict with economic demands. Women folk are expected to gather and begin preparing food at two-o-clock in the morning in time for a funeral that is due to begin at 6am. Many of these women have to be at work at 7am or 8am before they even see their children wake up. In a time of high crime it is dangerous for women to travel or walk the streets so early in the morning in many places. Women are pressurised and find it difficult to relax and enjoy cultural participation in such circumstances. Would not more shared responsibility between women and men enable everyone to enjoy cultural activities; after all are we not a sharing nation?

In multicultural South Africa it is recognised that all people have a right to their culture and beliefs to the degree that they do not impact negatively on others. The preamble to the constitution states that South Africa "belongs to all who live in it, united in our diversity". Additionally the Constitution's "Founding Provisions" recognises 11 official languages and must also promote Khoi, Nama and San languages as well as sign languages. The Constitution goes further still in promoting respect for "all languages commonly used by communities in South Africa, including German, Greek Gujarati, Hindi, Portuguese, Tamil, Telegu and Urdu, and Arabic, Hebrew, Sanskrit, and other languages used for religious purposes in South Africa."

Clearly then we are not allowed to be xenophobic. Nevertheless, suspicion of the stranger remains; I refer particularly to the black foreigner. Ought we not to treat these fellow Africans as we do fellow South Africans? It is common that ordinary human error is construed to be racially motivated. Fear of, the stranger (Ba tswa kwa), conflicts with the beautiful concept of Ubuntu botho (others make us people). Strangers should be welcomed as they were when they first came to our shores. We should remember that many nations are strengthened and developed by foreigners; indeed countries such as Australia, Canada, the United States, and New Zealand encourage immigration and see it as a vital part of their country's social and economic development. Our forefathers welcomed strangers, but I fear that this has now changed.

Today's youth meet the clash of cultures head on, often with dire consequences as they attempt to overcome the daily challenges and hurdles thrown up in their path. Taverns are mushrooming at an alarming rate. Drugs are easily obtainable on the streets. How can the youth escape such dangers? How are we to save our youth? The common proverbs are "charity begins at home" and "the home is the first teacher of the child". But how many parents realistically have the ability and the time to educate their children in these modern dangers? How much time do parents in fact have with their children today?

As I said above, with the removal of religious education from school, moral values and practice have declined. Pressure on youth to engage in sexual activity is unbearable. HIV/AIDS is on the rise. Most of those infected are among youth. The aged have to nurse and support the sick and dying when they ought to expect that the youth will care for them in their old age; this is how it is traditionally. Instead, as young people die at an alarming rate, old people are left to care for orphans.

The Actuarial Society of South Africa (ASSA) reported the total HIV/AIDS infections for South Africa in 2002 was 6 461 372. Of these, 6 141 578 were adults (18-64). Of these 3 016 080 were men (18-64); and 3 125 498 were women (18-64). There were 3 199 493 women of child-bearing age (15-49) infected with HIV/AIDS. Amongst the youth (15-24), 1 210 749 were infected with the virus. Of these 263 069 were male youths (15-24) and 947 680 female youths (15-24). The number of children (0-14) infected with HIV/AIDS was given as 205 134.

These figures for 2002 are challenging, but what are today's figures? How are we to lessen the burden on teenagers? Teenage pregnancy is escalating despite the fear of AIDS. Girls still in the classroom receive social grants to enable them to care for their child. In some schools when the grant is paid some classes are almost empty of girls.

The current emphasis on condoms poses a moral danger to the individual and society. There are of course a percentage of youth who abstain from sexual intercourse. But for others condoms seem to be a licence to indulge themselves. There is no message to connect sexual intercourse with family life. Condom use is the choice of males and they are freely promoted and available. 'Femodoms', however, do not appear to have the same commercial sponsorship. This would appear to promote the inequality of the sexes and support the common notion in South Africa that women are subject to men. While condoms are readily available so is abortion on demand if all else fails. The message to youth is Sex is ok as long as it's safe; safe from infection and safe from pregnancy. So much for moral regeneration!

# Reflections On The Past
# A Source Of Liberation

◆

The youth of the past often had to miss class, but not for the same reasons as today. They would be called upon to look after the cattle and goats and to care for their siblings. Such absences from school were not looked upon as an opportunity not to learn. Children absent from class would handle their responsibilities well, trying to catch-up on missed classes and managing to hand in their homework. In spite of these difficulties and the lack of opportunity for blacks under the apartheid government, the people still got teachers, nurses and other professionals who became good citizens, some outstanding.

In contrast, youth today, in principle, have open access to all careers. Unlike former generations black youth are advantaged by the policy of black empowerment that seeks to promote the most able in order to redress the imbalance created by policies of past regimes. The difficulties faced by today's youth are more diverse and complex than being commonly called to assist with livestock and siblings, such as alcohol and drug addiction, HIV/AIDS, pregnancy, the aftermath of abortion, not to mention inappropriate relationships between educators and learners, and the readiness of learners to resort to collective protest that leads on occasion to violent action; even burning down classrooms and other educational facilities on school property.

Of course in the past, there were young girls who fell pregnant, and such events raised eyebrows, but teenage pregnancy was rare. Girls were encouraged to remain virgins until they married, and wore with honour their white bridal gown.

Parents in the past were often less well educated than their children, but they held teachers in honour. Parental respect motivated teachers to commit themselves to the children in their charge. Today some educated parents seem to lack respect for the teaching profession and choose to ignore wider problems in society that influence the ability of children to learn. As children miss school classes, so parents miss parent meetings at school, often leaving attendance to grandparents who may find the complexities of the education system beyond them. Effective governance of schools requires a variety of skills; these are all too often lacking even in schools with professional parents (accountants, doctors, lawyers, health and social professionals) when elections for school governing bodies occur.

Parental vigilance and co-operation in enforcing school discipline is vital. Families have a decisive role to play in seeing that the values they teach their children at home are supported by schools. It is not unknown for strangers to hang around the vicinity of schools selling drugs to children, or for children to leave the school premises at lunchtime where there is an opportunity to buy alcohol that is returned to school undercover of a soft drink can. Food can be sold on school premises and school gates locked

Not so long ago children brought little or no money to school; they did not need it as they brought lunch boxes with them. Apart from ensuring a healthy diet, children had no money on their person for drugs and alcohol. The tendency today is to give even young children money to buy food, leaving them not only open to exploitation by outsiders, but to insiders too who may bully them for their cash.

The attractions of advertising that present values of success and happiness in terms of material acquisitions; such as flashy cars which are well beyond the reach of average households, the latest cell phone and computer technology, are a cause of great pressure on the youth. How can they be happy, how can they be a complete person if they do not have the latest car, cell phone and other gadgets? Perhaps this inadequacy accounts for the high rate of street crime, burglary, and car theft in South Africa? If the youth cannot afford luxury goods how other than by crime will they obtain them?

In the past, commercial advertising influence on moral values was negligible. Family and society managed to maintain acceptable standards of behaviour, and this in spite of the social and domestic division and disruption of apartheid which obliged parents to spend long periods of absence from home working in whites- only areas. The practical effect of parental absence gave rise to two sets of parents - Grandmother was known as Mme wa mo gae (my-mother-who-is-at-home), and our biological mother as, Mme wa kwa toropong (my-mother-who-is-in-town).

Traditional values were passed on to children not only through teaching and discipline, but through the story telling of grandmothers. Today children do not seem to have time to listen to grandparents as they socialise at the cinema and among friends at parties outside of the home. Or when at home sit in front of the television with the volume turned to maximum so they can hear what is said or sung over the blare of the CD player or radio perched above the television as they chat to their friends on their cell phones. Children today are never alone; they live by choice in a sea of noise in which the voices of grandparents are rarely heard.

Grandparents should take steps to ensure that their stories will be heard by recording them either in writing or orally. The liberating value of their tales lies in the fact that children's and society's sense of identity will be strengthened. This is why I write.

In the not too distant past it was unknown for races to mix in school. Today children from Reception to Grade 12 of different races may travel on the same bus to attend the same school; sit in the same classroom at the same desk following the same syllabus. They may use the same toilet facilities, and at boarding schools, use the same bathroom and sleep in the same dormitory, and use the same recreational facilities. Hopefully these acquaintances and friendships will flow on to university, college, and the workplace life. The conditions for our 'born-free' youth to mix and grow closer together are in place, and this is praiseworthy and to be encouraged, but not necessarily at the cost of widening the generation gap among their own people. Letlhaku le lesha le agelelwa mo go le legologolo ('new branches are built on top of old ones).

# Stereotypes
# Liberating Perceptions

◆

Generalisations about groups making up South African society need to be vehemently challenged. Stereotypes are rarely supported by bare facts; so for example the belief that whites are superior to blacks is not based upon verifiable data but upon ideology designed to maintain social and economic divisions and inequalities of one group over another. Likewise the conviction that men are intellectually superior to women is held in the face of the evidence where given equal schooling opportunities, girls regularly outperform boys in exam results. Moreover, single sex schools for girls commonly do better than those for boys.

In reality education is a complex mix of teaching and learning ability, social and economic factors among others. What may be said about grading of schools according to results however is that league tables give the lie to women being intellectually inferior to men.

In many groups, perhaps with the exception of matrilineal societies, the belief exists that men must be the sole breadwinner in the family, and any income the wife may earn ought to be managed by her husband. In reality the ideal in families is complementary. Husbands and wives each have a role to play in caring for the family through a partnership of those equal in dignity. In relationships where men believe they are socially superior to women, and where women are convinced they are socially inferior to men, conditions exist to maintain women in abusive relationships as women believe they cannot exist alone.

Much of the recent history of South Africa is a history of struggle, particularly against Apartheid, a political and legal system that promoted the interests of one group stereotyped by racial superiority over and against other groups stereotyped by racial inferiority. The danger today is that the youth will know little or nothing of this evil ideology and the great efforts it took to discredit and overthrow it. Worse still, the youth will not care less about the people on whose persistence and courage their present freedoms rest. Often youth give the impression that the current conditions they enjoy today were enjoyed by their parents and grandparents, and in the end, the past is not worth knowing. But youth must not forget, for the past is worth knowing if history is not to be repeated and undermine the efforts required of all South Africans to work for forgiveness and reconciliation. Great strides towards reconciliation have been made, in part facilitated by the Truth and Reconciliation Commission. The challenge is to maintain momentum.

Superiority complexes and inferiority complexes feed on stereotypes. Fortunately it would appear that many blacks are ceasing to measure themselves and other blacks against whites. Few black women have an English figure, so why do we worry. How often are such phrases, ba ja jaaka makgoa  they eat like white people; and ba ja dijô tsa makgoa  they eat the white people's food, heard today? And how often is the ngwana o tshwana le coloured she looks like a coloured sung at weddings today? Blacks who utter such phrases and sing such songs do not see themselves as beautiful or equal in God-given dignity with other races and groups. Many youth today sport clothing proclaiming 'black is beautiful', but not a few invest in complexion lightening cosmetics. We are beautiful as we are.

Stereotypes feed on fear; fear of the unknown; fear of the non-existent; and fear of what might be. People were warned of die rooi gevaar (the red danger), a term not only applicable to members of the Communist Party, but resistance fighters and those who opposed the apartheid regime even by peaceful means. Citizens, who were white, were also warned about die Romse gevaar the Roman Catholic Church in South Africa, because of its general support for the abolition of apartheid. Church members were labelled by the government of the day as communists. In reality die rooi and Romse gevaar, comprised people struggling to make their voices heard.  Small wonder then that in such a climate some saw armed resistance as legitimate. This was a time of little or no reflection. Policeman, white and black, did not apparently pause to reflect upon why some residents of South Africa had to be hunted day and night. The 'Most Wanted' were stereotyped as communists and terrorists by the regime; while the hunted called themselves socialists and freedom fighters.

In April 1994, Nelson Rolihlahla Mandela, who was to be president of the Republic of South Africa from 1994 to1997), said in his inaugural speech, with reference to the obvious harm resulting from the stereotypes generated by Apartheid: "Never again shall we allow oppression of one person or race against another." Perhaps the most significant political illustration in recent South African history of the breakdown of stereotypes occurred during the period of "floor crossings" in 2004. Martinus van Schalkwyk, leader of the National Party (NP), the party of Apartheid, dissolved itself in this process, and van Schalkwyk and others joined the African National Congress (ANC), the party of "terrorists", some of whom still struggle to obtain visas to enter Western countries because of their apartheid prison records and the "terrorist" labels.

*Maggie- Tshukudu Secondary School receiving a present from the Bafokeng King Lebone E. Molotlegi .*

# Liberated Captives

◆

Many citizens of South Africa live in two worlds: the scientific and technological world that seeks to offer rational and logical explanations of cause and effect of life's complex daily events, welcome and unwelcome, expected and unexpected; and the chaotic and often capricious world that seeks reasons hidden from ordinary people for the unexpected and often tragic occurrences that inflict themselves on the blameless and wicked on a regular basis.

One world is generally secure and explicable: the other uncertain, insecure and inexplicable. The degree of affiliation to these worlds varies according to the individual's inclination and commitment. Some live the greater part of their life in the rational and scientific world, only visiting the world of chaos and unpredictability occasionally and briefly. Others live permanently with a foot in both worlds. A minority choose to spend as little time in the world of science and technology as possible. Those citizens of South Africa, of whom there is not an insignificant number, who move frequently between these two worlds, are the liberated captives. Their influence on society limits the process of South African liberation.

Traditional healers have been around since time immemorial, but the arrival of whites at the Cape of Good Hope in 1652 initiated a conflict between western and ethnic medicine that remains unresolved. A major issue is pricing. Traditional healers tend to charge what the market will stand, and that people are willing to pay a R1000 or more for a consultation and treatment; and in some cases a herd of oxen suggests not only faith in the proficiency of the healer, but in their ability to communicate with the ancestors and therefore to indicate the reason for the illness and the person responsible. As no-one dies of natural causes; someone living or dead is always responsible; so no-one falls sick through contagion or natural causes, but through the agency of someone living or dead. On the other hand, a registered medical practitioner's charges are regulated by the Medical Council of South Africa and the government, about R150 for a consultation, and R200 to see a specialist. They also prescribe scientifically, careful to explain the dosage to patients, and are aware of the dangers of cross contamination and infection between patients they treat. In contrast to western practitioners, traditional healers display little appreciation of cross infection and little appreciation of an individual's tolerance and reaction to medication and dosage. The combination of peoples' loyalty in unregulated and unscientific methods, the unwillingness of traditional healers to reveal tricks of their trade, and the belief that treatment also relies on the co-operation of the ancestors, reinforces peoples reliance on the irrational and the unknown.

Taboos are an important part of life and respecting them ensures the continuation of harmony between people and ancestors. Some people however are inconsistent in their observance of these. There is a convention that pregnant women and young people must not enter a house or a room in which there is a newborn baby lest the baby will develop complications such as the delayed detachment of the umbilical cord, or will cry excessively, become restless and even die. The belief concerning a sick person is similar to that of the newborn baby. Family members place a log across the main door of the house. Seeing the log, people will not dare to cross the threshold. Ironically when a baby is born in hospital or a person lies seriously sick in hospital these taboos are ignored. Sick visits are paid irrespective of pregnancy, age and sex. Nurses, doctors, and cleaners may be male or female, young or old or even pregnant. No objections are made.

Particularly difficult in Tswana society is that of widows. A recently bereaved widow must mourn for as long as a year. During this period she may not visit friends; she is not supposed to touch us, and those who regarded her as a friend do not want her near their homes during this period. They allege the widow will be an ill-omen. We must all die one day. During mourning the widow is isolated and lonely: the very person in need of comfort is shunned by her friends. Where is ubuntu in this situation? Why do we not invite widows to visit?

In order to protect others, widows must use separate utensils, and no-one else may use them or touch them as they will be afflicted with bad luck. The only person who may come close to a recently bereaved widow is another widow whose task it is to serve her meals. Widow-to-widow-service protects women with husbands who if they came into contact with the widow might in their turn lose their husbands.

Of course the widow is not left entirely alone; there are family members who comfort her. But in their presence she must lie face down and look away from them. It is a generally taboo in many parts of the world to eat with the left hand. In the first period of mourning the widow must eat with her left hand and share her food with her lastborn, who likewise must consume food using the left hand.

As is the case with the sick and pregnant in hospitals, people come into daily contact with widows. They serve us in restaurants, in shops; they work as domestics and prepare food for their employers; they come to churches on Sundays. In these situations we come into physical contact with each other, yet nothing bad happens to us; we do not drop dead. Why do people not bother to establish the status of all women with whom they come into contact for fear they might be a widow in mourning? What is the difference between a wife losing her husband, and a mother losing a son or daughter? The former imposes isolation, the latter does not. Widows ought to wear black voluntarily, not by coercion. Does it matter if a widow mourns in private? Only it seems if she remains at home, but not if she works. Society should do everything possible to liberate widows from misery imposed from outside when they endure much misery by the loss of their husbands.

Many people living with ease in the rational, scientific and technological world of the 21st Century and still observe taboos such forbidding salt to enter or leave the house after sunset, but do not mind if after a long day's work salt finds its way into the house in the shopping bag after sunset. Likewise water must not enter the house after sunset, but it enters after sunset through taps in the kitchen and bathroom.

When farmers cry for rain in order to grow crops to feed the nation, somewhere else someone will be using a young girl to mix herbs to stop rain spoiling their wedding. Ironically such young girls study science at school and know the principles of cloud formations that make for rain.

# Liberating Our Neighbour: Enemy And Friend

◆

Witchcraft among black communities in South Africa has created many problems, not least the degree of trust between neighbours and even family members.

It is commonly said that nobody gets sick or dies of natural causes. Someone is always to blame. Who then can be trusted? People are prepared to pay amounts of money vastly disproportionate to their income to the Ngaka ya ditaola (the traditional healer and diviner) in order to discover the person responsible for the visitation of misfortune, ill health, or death. The culprit may be anyone with whom you do not have a good relationship; or someone with whom you had occasion to disagree; or someone you always suspected of jealousy towards yourself or family; or someone who sees you as a professional or social rival. On the other hand the perpetrator may turn out to be someone you never suspected or would ever suspect. For a price the Ngaka ya ditaola will cast the bones.

Among some groups in South Africa, revenge is immediate and public; in others, retribution comes by stealth. When lightening strikes and people or oxen are struck, the person responsible for sending the lightening must be sought out; the witch must be identified. Often retribution comes in the form of torching the alleged witch's house, and it is not unknown that the suspected witch herself is "necklaced" as well as her house torched. Commonly the identified witch is an old woman, often neglected by her family. If additionally she is considered ugly, then her revolting looks are taken as "positive proof" that she possesses occult powers. When the hunt is on, it has become general practice for old women to flee their homes and seek asylum in the local police station.

An additional complication generating anxiety is that a lightening strike is not what it appears to be; namely a bolt of lightening. The proverb says lightning does not strike twice in the same place. Lightning is cunning however; it is a bird that lays its eggs where it strikes. When someone comes along and discovers the lightning's eggs, it may maliciously strike again.

The family, like the family home, is a symbol of security. It is in the family and the home that we have our first experience of trust. Out of family trust and security we learn to be trustful of others and feel secure in their presence. By this process we are able to makeup our minds about people and gradually move out into the world and take our place as responsible and valuable members of society. This is the ideal.

When misfortune strikes, unfortunately, family members may be blamed for these unpleasant events: aunts, grandmothers and daughters-in-law are the alleged common culprits. The ngaka ya ditaola is often vague in identifying the person responsible for misfortune. He may not identify a specific person but generalise along such lines, for example: "The culprit is a woman, when she comes to your house the sun shines on her forehead." This simplification is useful to the person paying for the divination as it gives them the opportunity to name the person themselves from among the many acquaintances, visitors, and family members that fit such descriptions and take action against them. Or, the culprit may for an additional fee be punished by the traditional healer. In such cases the perpetrator often meets the same fate as their victim by the power of the Ngaka ya ditaola who has the power to turn the original curse against the person who originally laid it. It is interesting to note that the majority of those suspected of witchcraft are women. Little or nothing is heard of wizards. Those men and women who participate in divining the culprit create much stress for themselves and in the process generate mistrust of friend and stranger. Traditional healers grow fat on the proceeds of fear of the unknown.

Traditional healers also make money by employing their muti  medicine to ensure that the deceased rests in peace in the grave without being disturbed or exhumed by witches who in their turn may use their muti which might be used to kill the deceased's entire family.

People living in this world of suspicion and fear of neighbours also live in fear of nature and the natural world.  In summer, snakes move around seeking food and an environment to regulate their body temperature: on occasions snakes enter houses. There are those who do not believe that snakes enter dwellings accidentally, but enter with the purpose of killing a member of the household. Birds are known to fly in through open windows, particularly the Redwing Starling in this part of the world. A bird however does not fly into a room haphazardly, but by choice. Once in the house the bird is no longer seen as harmless: it is a nônyane ya baloi a "witch-bird". The evil snake and bird must be killed, for in killing the bird and snake the witch is also eradicated.

Baboons are associated with witchcraft. The sudden appearance of a baboon in a village or township sparks a hunt for its owner. In my childhood days in Moiletswane we could see the thieving baboons descending the mountains to dine on the fruits of our hard work. Boys would chase them from the mielie fields. Driving baboons away was dangerous, not because of witchcraft, but because it was not unknown for large baboons to turn on young boys pursing them. Somehow or other we never associated baboons with evil; only with hunger.

Mistrust of others is harmful and can result in psychosis that may lead to actions that in other circumstances someone would not execute. For example, a son kills his mother with an axe and claims it was an act of self defence. The son did not see his mother but rather a large vicious dog that was about to tear him to pieces. He struck with the axe several times and successfully killed the ferocious beast. It was only after the act that the son realised he had killed his mother.

What measures can we take to liberate ourselves and society from the anxiety and fear of witchcraft? Firstly, we can begin by actively caring for the frail and aged. People in very old age are not always aware of what they are saying or doing. They may wander off and forget the way home or even stray into strangers' houses and risked being stereotyped as the intrusive snake or bird. Sometimes old people wonder off naked. Nakedness is associated with witchcraft. Cries of "witch, witch" by startled householders only aggravate their confusion and anxiety about being lost. Little wonder then that such people are incoherent and behave strangely putting themselves at risk of a severe beating or even death.

In essence, people not only associate witchcraft with danger to themselves and the group, but as a potent means of self-protection; often protection against death. The fact is however, that we must all die. In our efforts to come to terms with death we do not see dieing as a natural part of life's process, and against all experience we treat death irrationally, as something that could have been prevented.

As I said, only a few die of natural causes. But the end of all living things in this world is death. Trees die, grasses die, and animals die. Humans meet death in a variety of ways, old age, sickness, road accidents and homicide. We fear death; even our funeral practices and rites show this particularly if the death is unexpected or violent. If someone dies accidentally some believe the corpse must not come into the house before being taken to the place of burial. This measure is to protect family members, for the belief is that others of the family will follow one another in the same manner if the deceased is brought into the home. For this reason, church services are conducted outside the yard near the gate. Or, the corpse is left outside the gate and the service is conducted in a tent in the yard. So it is that as a result of dieing in an accident a loved one suddenly becomes a stranger in his or her own home. Is it within our power to determine that we should not die accidentally?

Communities and individuals can assist the elderly by being good neighbours: doing small kindnesses and services such as laundry, shopping, collecting prescriptions from the pharmacy, bringing them meals, taking them to the doctors as and when necessary. This is preferable to paying for an expensive funeral at which a quantity of food is consumed that would have fed the deceased for a year as well as driving to the funeral in expensive cars that could have transported the old when they were alive. Rather than display our public love for someone it is preferable to show them love discreetly in their living years.

*My elder sister - Midah, her daughter, Yvonne and my mother, Martha. Seated in front is Kgomotso, my sister's grandson.*

# Liberating Memory

◆

The country of South Africa into which I was born in 1939 was very different to the South Africa of today, and that of my children and grandchildren. Much of my life has been spent among a society which insisted on the sharp distinctions between races, nations and peoples. These differences were enshrined in law, and for just over four decades under successive Nationalist governments, these laws were enforced vigorously and often viciously by a people who considered themselves superior purely on the grounds of colour white, which is arguably not a colour at all! During my life I have known and experienced discrimination not only between whites and blacks but between blacks and blacks.

Men often treated women harshly, considering themselves superior on account of gender. With some exceptions, black politicians, civil servants and police, of the homelands oppressed their own people at the behest of racist Apartheid governments and on account of self-interest. Black functionaries of the Apartheid regime, themselves of the oppressed classes, enforced the oppression of their own people.

But I have also been blessed to live through a period that led to positive change in South Africa, and to which I am proud to have made a contribution. Christina Rossetti (1830-1894), wrote in her poem, Remember: "Better by far you should forget and smile that you should remember and be sad." This is rarely sound advice, and certainly not so in our case. Nelson Mandela calls ours a 'Rainbow Nation'. The visible colours of the rainbow are wonderfully and beautifully distinct, but the demarcations between the various colours are not sharply drawn, rather they are imprecisely rendered. After a shower of rain, against the backdrop of the sun, we see each band of colour clearly, and we notice how their borders gently merge, the one bleeding into the other.

The process of merging internal borders of South African society is a new and fragile project. Here, I have recorded some memories, happy and sad, from my life. They are a contribution to the softening of boundaries between distinctive South African cultures, races, and peoples so that I, my children, grandchildren, you, and future generations may not harbour bitterness and deep hurts of old; may not forget the past, but may all live, each confident and secure in his or her own culture, as a people of hope, co-operating with one another and finding our unity and strength in our diversity. And in so doing, be an example that makes a hopeful contribution - that is distinctly South Africa - to justice, peace and the common good of people the world over.

"What a strange thing is memory, and hope; one looks backward, the other forward. The one is of today, the other is the tomorrow. Memory is history recorded in our brain, memory is a painter, it paints pictures of the past and of the day." - *Grandma Moses, My Life's History.

*Grandma Moses (Anna Mary Robertson Moses; 18601961), United States primitive painter, largely self-taught whose paintings are characterised by the harmonious arrangements of people.

*My mother, Martha in her grand church uniform.*